TAKE YOUR VICTORIES AS THEY COME

THE CARLSON YEARS IN MINNESOTA POLITICS

FOREWORD BY CLEM HASKINS
EDITED BY MARY LAHR SCHIER

MSP
BOOKS

Minneapolis, MN

220 South Sixth Street, Suite 500
Minneapolis, MN 55402

DESIGNED BY JULIE DIXON

JACKET PHOTOGRAPHY BY MARK LUINENBURG

CAPITOL PHOTOGRAPHY BY ANTHONY BRETT SCHRECK

Printed in the United States of America

Library of Congress Catalog Card Number 98-67546

ISBN 0-9641908-3-4

Many people have contributed to the success of the Carlson administration. I will always owe each of them the highest degree of gratitude. Among the countless hardworking Minnesotans who stood with me to make our state better and stronger, I would like to extend special thanks to my wife, Susan, and my children, Anne, Tucker, and Jessica. Anne, in particular, deserves special tribute. Despite serious illnesses, her relentless dedication, infectious enthusiasm and unwillingness to ever give up have inspired all who know her. Thank you, Anne, Tucker, Jessica, and Susan for your devotion, your commitment, and your love.

TABLE OF CONTENTS

FOREWORD

By Clem Haskins

The year was 1986, and I was the new men's basketball coach at the University of Minnesota. Having taken this job on the heels of one of the program's most tumultuous years, I began my tenure with a certain amount of trepidation and anxiety. The basketball program had a long way to go and a great deal of recovering to do, and there was no way we could accomplish this without the strong support of true fans and good friends. It was at that time that I met a man who was to be both: Arne Carlson.

Arne was state auditor at that time, and our long friendship began with letters of encouragement that he wrote to me, my staff, and my players. At a time when very few people had positive things to say about the Gophers basketball team, Arne's warm and human letters buoyed the spirits and the confidence of both new players and veterans alike.

When the season began, we were faced with one-sided losses and miniscule crowds. I was literally walking up and down University Avenue giving away tickets to our games. Loyal fans were few and far between, but I could always count on seeing Arne and Susan in their maroon-and-gold sweaters, shouting encouragement to our players and "advice" to the referees. And, believe me, the players took notice as well. From veterans like Ray Gaffney, Tim Hanson, and David Holmgren, who had kept the program going as part of the scrappy "Iron Five," to awkward incoming freshman like Willie Burton and Kevin Lynch, the players were well aware and very appreciative of the unbridled enthusiasm and support of Arne Carlson.

Over the following years, as the success of our program was built and solidified, so too was my relationship with Arne and Susan Carlson. More than just fans, they became true friends and confidantes to my wife, Yevette and me, my coaches, and our players. When Arne became Governor, nothing changed. He was still at every game, still calling me and dropping notes of encouragement to our players, still living and dying with every victory or loss. The nice thing was, this wasn't just some front-runner politician jumping on the bandwagon of success. This was a true fan who had been with us when things were at their worst.

It has been a great delight to have Governor Carlson as a fan. Whether it's been having the team to his home for dinner, giving a pregame pep talk, or traveling with us to the Final Four, Arne is always there for the Gophers. His support for the team is surpassed only by his devotion to the University itself. You could see that as he fought passionately for the record-setting U of M bonding bill passed in 1998. Arne knows that sports are just a part of the picture in the ultimate overall success at the University of Minnesota.

Theodore Roosevelt celebrated the individual who participated in the arena of life. That is Arne in a nutshell. His induction into the University of Minnesota's Hall of Fame is a very rare honor and fully deserved. He truly loves everything in Minnesota and, not only has he been the "sixth man" for Gopher Basketball, but he has also been a true friend.

Clem Haskins
July 1998

TAKE YOUR VICTORIES AS THEY COME

Introduction

A steel gray, early winter day enveloped Minnesota as the state airplane climbed through the clouds, returning Governor Arne Carlson to St. Paul from St. Cloud. It was one more short hop in a small plane, just like many others the governor took in his eight years in office. Above the thrum of the 10-seater's engines, conversation drifted to one of Arne Carlson's passions: World War II history.

Press Secretary Jackie Renner, a former television reporter who covered the strange 1990 election that put Carlson in office, had been reading *The Man Called Intrepid*, a true story of spies and intrigue. Carlson nodded. He also had read the book.

"Do you remember the part about the English village and the codes?" Renner asked. Carlson shook his head, and Renner explained the dilemma faced by Allied Intelligence agents before the United States entered World War II. The English had broken a Nazi code and the intelligence officers knew that the Germans planned a bombing raid on a small English village. The question was, should they evacuate the village and risk the Nazis figuring out that they knew the code, or should they let the village be bombed in hopes of gathering more important information later? They never warned the villagers.

"Big mistake," Carlson said. "Huge mistake."

"Why?" Renner asked. "They didn't want the Nazis to know they had the code."

"Outside of the moral issues of letting those people be bombed, it was a strategic mistake," Carlson said. "You don't put things off because you hope to get something better later. You take your victories as they come. You don't save it for tomorrow because tomorrow there will always be something else."

It's a philosophy Carlson embraced for 30 years in politics and public life. Don't hesitate. Know where you want to go and take the advantages events give you.

Carlson's willingness to take risks was at the root of his success as governor, but it was not the only reason for his success. Repeatedly Carlson's supporters and opponents pointed to three reasons. First, he was the right governor at the right time. In 1991, Minnesota needed a fiscal conservative to manage the state's finances as it worked its way out of a recession. It also needed a governor who could guide the state through the transformations all states faced in the early 1990s as the federal government pushed social programs back to the states. The situation Carlson inherited in 1991 was filled with challenges, but they were challenges he was well suited to meet.

Second, the governor slowly built a middle-ground coalition in Minnesota. The state's political parties remained strongholds of the conservative and liberal extremes. But in the Minnesota Legislature and among voters, Carlson forged alliances to promote his agenda on issues ranging from the environment to school choice.

Finally, the governor took his politics personally. The issues on which he was most successful were ones he cared about personally and deeply: fiscal restraint, education, building the state's economy, and finding ways to improve the lives of children in Minnesota. For these issues, Arne Carlson took risks, and he took his victories as they came.

CHAPTER ONE

THE UNFORGETTABLE CAMPAIGN

Carlson Emerges to Win a Goofy Gubernatorial Election

An unlikely group of protesters milled around the gates of the Governor's Residence on the Saturday evening before the 1990 election. A buttoned-down crowd of Republicans of the most moderate sort paraded in front of the Summit Avenue mansion, struggling to keep their candles from burning out in the November chill. They were business owners, housewives, and students, caught up in the excitement of an improbable campaign for governor. This was a group more likely to show up at PTA meetings and Chamber of Commerce lunches than political protests.

Still, they chanted for an appearance by incumbent Governor Rudy Perpich, imploring him to come out of the castle and debate Arne Carlson. The group feebly sang, "We Shall Overcome." No one really expected Perpich to emerge; rather it was an event staged to draw attention to Perpich's refusal to debate Carlson, the last-minute nominee of the Republican Party.

Carlson arrived with a squadron of media people behind him.

Carlson pulled one of his supporters aside. "What the heck do

I say if the guy comes out?"

The protesters decided not to linger too long. Carlson gave a brief talk, then led his supporters in the "Minnesota Rouser." The vigil ended with no sign of Perpich, but it had achieved its goal. Carlson and his unlikely campaign would be on television that night. For his supporters, the vigil reminded them of how much fun politics could be. They had already seen defeat in the primary. To be there at all, to have a chance at the governorship, was more than Carlson or his supporters expected. One supporter described life before the 1990 campaign as unfolding like a black-and-white movie. Life during those crazy two weeks exploded in Technicolor. "I have never felt as alive and as synthesized as I did in those two weeks," the supporter said.

It was an election like no other, though it started the way every campaign does—with a small group of people, a candidate, and a feeling of hope. For Kris Sanda, a long-time Republican activist, the 1990 campaign started in the hallway of an apartment building in New Brighton, where she was living. It was 1988. Arne Carlson had asked if she would meet with him and an aide. As she unlocked the security door to let them in, Sanda asked, "Is it about the governor's race?"

"Yes," Carlson said, and smiled broadly. Sanda was relieved. She'd been hoping Carlson would run in 1990. While he had a reputation among Republicans as a maverick, he also had great intelligence, the ability to bring a crowd to its feet, and an understanding of government. She had already decided Carlson was the only Republican who could win the governorship from Rudy Perpich—a view Perpich shared. Sanda organized Carlson's first committee, a group of moderate Republicans including many who had worked with Carlson in Minneapolis politics since the mid-1960s. The group that met throughout 1988 and 1989 included former county attorney Gary Flakne; former state Senator Joe O'Neill; Fred Krohn, who worked in the auditor's office; banker Joe Kingman; attorney Vince Ella and his wife, Kathy; party activists Myra Peterson and Pat Jilk; and Carlson's long-time campaign ad man, Conrad "Connie" Razidlo. It was a "rag-tag band," according to one member.

The group hoped to capitalize on the efforts of Bob Dole's presidential campaign in Minnesota in 1988. The group also felt that the same moderate Republicans who helped Dole could be organized around Carlson. They used the Dole campaign mailing list to identify progressive Republicans. Unfortunately for these early supporters, the moderates were moderate in many ways, including in their propensity to make large political contributions.

Late in 1989, Kingman and O'Neill planned a fund-raiser for Carlson among their St. Paul business associates. They invited about 150 Republican business owners. Four showed up. Jon Grunseth, a lobbyist for Ecolab, Inc., already had "sewn up every dollar in St. Paul," Kingman recalled. Grunseth's campaign for governor focused on entrepreneurs and others with "new money" who would support a more conservative candidate. The strategy worked. In 1989, the Grunseth campaign raised $254,000 to Carlson's $61,000. Businessman David Printy had also raised over a quarter of a million dollars in his bid for the governorship.

Carlson needed to make a change. So he called his brother Lars, who ran a division of H.B. Fuller Company. At lunch at a Perkins restaurant near Fuller's Shoreview campus, Arne explained that his campaign was broke and going nowhere. He asked his brother to help. Lars had not been active in Republican politics for several years, though he'd worked on Senator David Durenberger's 1978 campaign. He also had a personal consideration. Jon Grunseth was a good friend.

Lars determined that the campaign needed a professional staff, an outside consultant, and a lot more money. For the money, he went first to George Pillsbury and Wheelock Whitney, two well-established and well-heeled businessmen whose moderate politics and pro-choice beliefs made Grunseth an unlikely recipient of their support. Between them, they knew nearly every significant Republican contributor in Minnesota. The younger Carlson also recruited other operatives, like Paul Anderson, an attorney in the politically connected South St. Paul firm of LeVander, Gillen & Miller.

Within a couple of months, fund-raising improved, and the campaign soon established a headquarters at Twin City Towing on Jackson Street near the state Capitol, which was owned by state Representative Dick Pellow and his wife, Jean. The Pellows offered the campaign space, coffee cups, and any other supplies it needed. With its constant stream of tow trucks into the property, the campaign headquarters earned the affectionate nickname, "The Junkyard." Money was still tight, but a full-time manager, Kathy Ella, began organizing supporters and volunteers. Carlson's wife, Susan, shut down her law practice and joined the campaign as scheduler.

"We were doing the right things," said Lars Carlson. "The problem was they should have been done a year earlier."

Carlson faced political challenges as well. Minnesota's Independent Republican Party had moved increasingly to the right over the past decade. The chances of the party endorsing a moderate, pro-choice candidate like Carlson at its June convention were nil. Carlson opted not to seek party endorsement.

But the campaign had a small presence at the convention. During that time, a Carlson aide visited a gathering of the League of Minnesota Cities, which was meeting nearby. The aide went to check out Red Wing Mayor Joanell Dyrstad, Carlson's top choice for a running mate. Carlson had been impressed with Dyrstad when his office audited the books in Red Wing, where she was mayor. She was personable, knew the issues that mattered to local governments, and, most important, was a fervent Carlson supporter.

The Republican convention proved a contentious affair, with conservatives Printy and Grunseth battling for the nomination. Moderate Doug Kelley, an attorney and former Green Beret, sought the nomination but did not expect to get it. He surprised the largely pro-life delegates with a well-reasoned speech on the abortion issue. The pro-choice Kelley did not get their endorsement, but he earned the delegates' respect.

The endorsement went to Grunseth and the primary campaign began in earnest. A lack of money continued to hamper organizational efforts. Carlson hired Ruth Grendahl, to take over as campaign manager after the convention. On her first day in the office, only $200 in contributions arrived.

Despite the shortage of cash, the campaign frequently told the media that Carlson had "a million dollars worth of name recognition." This was half true. Because of his long tenure in politics, more than 80 percent of Minnesotans recognized Carlson's name. The majority had a favorable impression of the auditor, newspaper polls showed. The campaign team decided to capitalize on their candidate's superior name identification and use advertising—as opposed to get-out-the-vote efforts—to turn out the all-important middle-of-the-road voters.

"We all bought into that decision because we did not have a hard core of supporters to do phoning and we couldn't afford to buy phoners like Grunseth could," Anderson recalled. The campaign developed a series of issue-based advertisements with a positive tone.

The advertising assumed Carlson voters perceived Carlson as a good-government moderate. The ads never clearly defined who he was or why he would be a good governor. They also failed to delineate the differences between Carlson and Grunseth. With polls showing Carlson leading Grunseth by 20 percentage points, the campaign felt confident in staying with a positive message.

Signs of trouble emerged in late August. The campaign began getting calls from friends of Carlson. Many of these long-time Republicans had been telephoned once, twice, or three times by Grunseth phone banks to encourage them to vote for the conservative candidate. "Where's your get-out-the-vote effort?" they asked. In the final two weeks of the campaign, Grunseth unleashed a barrage of highly focused ads that compared Carlson and Grunseth on abortion, crime, and education. Using votes Carlson had cast as a legislator nearly 20 years earlier, they portrayed Carlson as soft on crime and carrying a "liberal education agenda."

Carlson cried foul, but the campaign did not have enough money to respond effectively through television. Still, the polls showed Carlson with a substantial advantage and many of the campaign's leaders thought they would pull out a victory. When the results came in the evening of September 11, however, Grunseth had trounced both Carlson and Doug Kelley. The depressed crowd at the Thunderbird Inn in Bloomington watched as Carlson won only one Minnesota county, Joanell Dyrstad's home base in Goodhue County. Carlson got only 32 percent of the vote, to Kelley's 17 percent and Grunseth's 50 percent.

Carlson was stunned. "We didn't see it coming," he said. "The truth of the matter is that we ran a campaign that was largely 1960ish. We did candidate appearances, debates, citizen juries, editorial endorsements, and all the things you do to get broad-based support. We did that campaign well. But technology had changed things, technology based on single-issue politics. Now, through telephoning, you could mobilize those single-issue groups that are a key factor in primary elections. We ran a generalist campaign, while the opposition built a very sharply focused campaign around two groups: the antiabortion groups and the National Rifle Association. Those groups show up in a primary.

"Looking back on it, you could ask the question, why were we so stupid?"

GETTING ON WITH LIFE

Rudy Perpich called Carlson the morning after the primary election loss. The governor expressed condolences—and relief. He had long considered Carlson his most formidable Republican foe. Perpich advised Carlson to get on with his life and perhaps even get a job overseas, as Perpich himself had once done after his defeat in 1978. As a gesture of kindness, Perpich invited Carlson to a reception for visiting members of the British Parliament.

"I remember going to the Governor's Residence," Carlson recalled, "and thinking this is the last time I'll see this place."

At a meeting eight days after the primary, the campaign committee discussed how to close down the Carlson campaign and retire about $50,000 in debt. Although several pro-choice groups had been urging Carlson to consider a write-in, no one on the committee thought Carlson could win that way.

Campaign Treasurer Bob Ferderer brought up one extra item at the meeting. During the primary campaign, Ferderer, a retired 3M executive and pro baseball scout, had earned a reputation as a man who took care of the smallest details. The campaign had received many contributions just before the election. Those needed to be recorded. He also wanted to make sure the campaign filed the proper forms with the Ethical Practices Board to preserve Carlson's ability to run in future elections. They needed to file the paperwork by the end of the month and Ferderer wanted the committee to sign off on it. Thinking it was another Ferderer obsession, the committee instructed him to file whatever papers he liked.

"I had a hard time accepting that Arne had lost," Ferderer said. "I just couldn't bring myself to shut down the campaign completely, not while people were talking about a write-in."

Ferderer and several others from the campaign maintained contact with a group calling itself Minnesotans for the Write Choice. Almost from the day after the election, they had been urging Carlson to continue as a write-in candidate. The group seemed to include only about a dozen people, said one Carlson supporter who met with them. They had no resources, except the ability to gain news coverage, but they kept Carlson's name before voters.

TAKING A CHANCE

On Monday, October 15, the gubernatorial campaign—which had been relatively dull—suddenly exploded into coffee shop and water cooler conversations all over the state. The *Star Tribune* printed explosive allegations about Grunseth's past. Voters might not comprehend or care about a state budget crisis, but everybody understood the alleged improprieties. Former Governor Elmer L. Andersen called for Grunseth to withdraw from the race. Minnesotans for the Write Choice organized rallies outside the auditor's office in St. Paul. "Run, Arne, run," they shouted. In one day, more than 200 people called Carlson's office urging him to run. Republican Party leaders were split on whether the Grunseth campaign could be salvaged.

Carlson and his supporters began to talk about reviving the campaign. None of them believed Grunseth could survive the allegations. Staying in the race only assured a Perpich victory. Because the Carlson campaign had not been totally dismantled, it would be simple to revive it. The papers Bob Ferderer had insisted on filing gave Carlson the right to state funding should he reenter the race. The campaign's databases and other computerized information were still easily available.

Under constant pressure from the media, Arne Carlson drove to his cabin in Wisconsin that Thursday. He needed solitude. During the two-hour drive, Carlson considered whether he could win a two-week campaign. Up to 35 percent of Minnesotans were still undecided about the gubernatorial race. These voters felt frustrated and unimpressed with both Perpich and Grunseth. To capture them, the campaign would have to act quickly and could not wait for Grunseth to step aside. He needed to act quickly to be positioned in voters' minds as the best—if not the only—alternative to a damaged candidate. What's more, the titillating nature of the charges against Grunseth had galvanized the attention of voters. The press would carry the campaign's message. For once, money would not be an overriding factor.

He decided he could do it. He had nothing to lose but two weeks of his life.

Back in the Twin Cities, Paul Anderson, Lars Carlson, and Len Hardwick, a Minneapolis marketing consultant who had been part of Carlson's initial group of supporters, met to ponder the same decision. They too decided that Arne could win it.

They gathered a larger group together the next night to develop plans with Arne Carlson. They formed the nucleus of the second campaign: Sanda; former legislator Craig Shaver; party operative Lois Mack; long-time political strategist Bob Anderson; Scott Day, a lobbyist from the Minnesota Education Association who had worked for the campaign before the primary; press secretary David Sampsel; Joanell and Marvin Dyrstad; and several others. All of them wanted to get started again; many had a sense they were about to make history.

That night, the group agreed to proceed with a write-in campaign, though they hoped for a Grunseth withdrawal. They planned to announce Carlson's candidacy on Tuesday or Wednesday.

The next morning, Lars Carlson got a call from Jann Olsten, campaign chair for U.S. Senator Rudy Boschwitz. Boschwitz's campaign had been running tracking polls throughout the past week and they showed that Grunseth's troubles were hurting all Republicans, including the two-term senator. Olsten wanted to know Carlson's plans, especially in light of a rumor that Doug Kelley planned to reenter the race. Lars agreed to meet with Olsten and Boschwitz campaign manager Tom Mason at the office of Wheelock Whitney that afternoon.

Kelley presented an unexpected roadblock. He was an attractive candidate. He had impressed many party regulars at their convention that summer with his speech on abortion. Because he had sought endorsement, party regulars might prefer Kelley to Carlson. But Kelley had no record as an elected official and no significant campaign organization. Few voters even recognized his name.

As the four men discussed the situation, Lars Carlson acknowledged that Arne Carlson planned to announce in the next day or so. Don't wait, Whitney counseled. He should get in today.

"I'll run the campaign, if you raise the money," Lars Carlson replied. Whitney agreed. Then Lars called his brother. They decided to announce that afternoon that Arne Carlson was entering the race as a write-in candidate. Ruth Grendahl hastily organized supporters for the announcement and more than a hundred people screamed and shouted at the news.

Whitney's advice saved Carlson's bid for governor. Not only did Carlson backers preempt Kelley's entrance into the race, but they announced one day before the *Star Tribune* of Minneapolis released a poll showing Grunseth within six percentage points of Perpich. Despite a week of lurid accusations and criticism, Grunseth still had the support of 40 percent of voters to Perpich's 46 percent. The same polls showed that with Carlson as a write-in, Perpich received 37 percent of the vote; Carlson and

Grunseth got 28 percent each. If Carlson had waited even until the next morning to announce, Grunseth's supporters could have argued convincingly that Grunseth could win the race and Carlson was a spoiler.

"I'm in," Arne Carlson said to the screaming crowd outside the state auditor's office.

"It was a resurrection," remembered Joe Kingman. "This had happened only once before."

"The guy had been shot and buried," said Craig Shaver. "He was looking at oblivion and then he had this terrific groundswell of support."

The campaign quickly re-established its headquarters at Twin City Towing. Mary Thomas, Carlson's secretary for 12 years, brought a computer from home and brought in her 11-year-old son to show her how to operate it. He joined the campaign, as did thousands of other Minnesotans caught up in the excitement of Carlson's renaissance.

Whatever the campaign needed suddenly appeared. Transportation? A dozen pilots donated planes, fuel, and time. Lawn signs? People made their own. Money? It was everywhere. Volunteers distributing literature in malls and downtown St. Paul returned to the Junkyard with checks that passersby had stuffed in their pockets. Some people even used the drive-through window at Twin City Towing to drop off checks. At one point, cash flowed into the campaign at a rate of over $40,000 a day. Almost a quarter of a million dollars—half of what Carlson had raised for the primary—came in during the week after his announcement. Direct mail? Nancy Brataas, a Rochester-based advertising executive and state legislator, developed a piece that could be put in the mail to arrive just before the election. Advertising? Connie Razidlo, Carlson's former ad man, pulled together freelancers to produce quick-turnaround television and radio spots. The campaign had so many volunteers that it did not have enough work for them. Not wanting to turn away any supporters, the campaign bought boxes of envelopes and mailing lists and put people to work addressing envelopes they would eventually throw away.

On the road, crowds greeted Carlson wildly at nearly every stop.

"It was such an extraordinary outpouring of support," he recalled. "I have never seen the likes of it. I would say, 'I want to get the campaign back to the issues,' and the crowds would scream and yell. I never actually got to talk about the issues."

He traveled constantly during the two weeks, visiting every major town in Minnesota. Lars ran the inside operation, spending nearly 20 hours a day at headquarters, "usually with two phones in my ear." At 7:30 A.M., the campaign's core held a meeting they called "the drill." Lars "fired off orders like an Uzi machine gun," one staffer recalled, as they determined how the day's events would unfold and assigned tasks to volunteers. Each drill ended with a brisk handclap and Lars' shout, "Let's rock and roll."

The campaign printed stickers and produced one television advertisement, which was never shown, to instruct voters on how to vote for a write-in candidate. The campaign also prepared for its first court case, seeking a ruling that did not require voters to write in both Carlson and Dyrstad's name. The campaign even came up with the idea to use "deer stand" to help people remember the lieutenant governor candidate's name. Even as the write-in campaign continued, insiders felt Carlson could not win that way. The effort, however, positioned Carlson as the Republicans' best alternative should Grunseth resign.

Three days after Carlson entered the race, it seemed that moment had come. Grunseth's campaign had signaled a major announcement. Everyone expected Grunseth would pull out of the race that evening.

A little before 10:00 P.M. that night, Jon Grunseth ripped up his resignation speech and announced he was staying in the race. The Carlson workers went back to mailing stickers.

Investigations into Grunseth's personal life continued. On Sunday, the *Star Tribune* carried another damaging story. Sunday evening, Arne Carlson was home in Shoreview, enjoying a few minutes of family time during the hectic campaign. As he peeled potatoes for supper, he heard the news that Grunseth had pulled out of the race.

COURTING VOTERS

The campaign now split into two fronts: The courtroom, where the campaign had to fight to get Carlson and Dyrstad's name on the ballot, and the court of public opinion.

From the first moment a second campaign seemed possible, Paul Anderson had begun studying the Minnesota statutes that governed elections. The statutes allowed parties to replace their nominee if a candidate could not stand for election. The law set out a three-step process. If the nominee could not stand, a "qualified committee" of the party could nominate someone else. If a qualified committee could not meet, then the second-place finisher in the primary election would become the candidate. If that was not possible, voters could petition to put a candidate on the ballot. The campaign recruited lawyers to work on each of the three questions, and, as an insurance policy, it collected the 2,500 signatures necessary to get Carlson on the ballot by petition.

The campaign already was scheduled to go before the Supreme Court that Tuesday—a week before the election—to present arguments in the case over whether both Carlson and Dyrstad's names had to be written in on a write-in vote. Earlier, Secretary of State Joan Growe, a Democrat, had ruled that both names needed to appear on the ballot or the vote was invalid. The ruling would surely cost the campaign thousands of votes. The campaign argued that because the two ran as a team, under Minnesota law, a vote for Carlson was automatically a vote for Dyrstad. At 10:00 A.M. Tuesday, Bruce Willis, a long-time Republican lawyer and election-law expert, presented the Carlson write-in case. The campaign hoped it would be moot by that evening.

Willis had contacted the Independent-Republican Party's attorney, Barry Anderson, to discuss the legal issues. Willis contended that nothing in the party's bylaws or constitution anticipated this incident. Willis, who had assisted Republicans in several election law disputes, urged Anderson to recommend that the party's executive committee concede that it had no qualified committee that could meet in time to select a candidate to replace Grunseth. The executive committee of the party saw

Perpich as vulnerable and did not want to waste this opportunity to win the governorship.

With supporters of Carlson and pro-life protesters outside, the executive committee met for three hours Tuesday night at party headquarters in Bloomington. Recalled Lars Carlson, "It wasn't very uncomfortable. I was ushered in and ushered out and that was it." In the end, the committee decided to certify to Joan Growe that it had no qualified committee to select a new candidate. Under state law, Carlson would go on the ballot.

Wilma Grams, a conservative party leader from Hutchinson, expressed the pragmatism that had overcome the party when she told reporters, "You have to go with what you have."

But the committee did not endorse Joanell Dyrstad because of another brewing intraparty dispute. When Grunseth resigned, he resigned alone. His lieutenant governor candidate, Sharon Clark, never officially took her name off the ballot. Many conservatives wanted Carlson to accept Clark as a running mate as a gesture of unity.

Dyrstad offered to quit the ticket. "Getting you elected is the most important thing," she told Carlson as they drove to a campaign event that evening.

He refused to change running mates and told the press that he didn't think even he could vote for a cobbled-together ticket like Carlson/Clark. He promised that Clark and other conservatives would have a role in his administration. "But make no mistake," he said. "The journey is with Dyrstad." The Supreme Court agreed to hear the second case Thursday afternoon.

The disarray in the Republican Party and the court battles took a toll on the campaign's efforts with voters too. Many voters felt disenchanted with politicians generally, but the campaign's polls showed these voters blamed the Republicans more than the Democrats. While the campaign's lawyers fought to get Carlson on the ballot, the election was slipping away.

Perpich's strength stemmed from the strong Democratic voting tradition of Minnesotans. Nearly 45 percent of the voters in Minnesota in 1990 considered themselves Democrats. Perpich needed only a few percentage points from Independents and

Republicans to win. For Carlson, winning a general election required that he pick up nearly all of the core Republicans (just under 35 percent of the electorate), carry independents by a wide margin, and garner votes from disenchanted Democrats.

"It was never a cakewalk," said marketing consultant Len Hardwick. "We had to do things just right or we lost." On Halloween, a Wednesday night, a large fund-raiser for Carlson was held at the 50th floor restaurant of the IDS Center in downtown Minneapolis. Before going into the building, Paul Anderson and Len Hardwick conferred on the street corner.

"We're losing this to Rudy," Hardwick said. They needed something to remind voters of why Rudy Perpich had to go. After all, the governor's approval rating had sunk to 36 percent earlier in the year, his lowest ever. As the two men walked into the IDS, they talked about developing a television ad to remind voters that Rudy Perpich had overstayed his welcome. The reception was packed. The excitement of the Carlson campaign had energized moderate Republicans.

With no place to sit, Hardwick went into the men's room. Taking a few sheets of paper from his briefcase, he sat by the sink and sketched out an ad that asked voters "Do you really want four more years of Rudy Perpich?" Connie Razidlo was ready at Northwest Teleproductions to flesh out the ad and produce it immediately.

The 30-second ad, called "Think About It," ended by saying "four more years of Perpich may seem like forever"—as the word forever stretches out into blackness. As he waited for the ad to be produced, Razidlo met Pat Forceia, campaign advisor to Paul Wellstone's Senate campaign against Rudy Boschwitz.

"After this election, there'll be no more Rudys," Forceia predicted.

Despite simple production, the ad delivered the right message at the right time. It began running almost immediately and, because the campaign finally had adequate cash, Razidlo purchased every time spot available to run it.

"Many voters did not know what Carlson stood for," Hardwick said. "They knew he wasn't Perpich and he wasn't Grunseth.

That was all they needed to know."

Thursday afternoon, the campaign was back in the courtroom again to argue *Clark v. Growe*, Sharon Clark's challenge to Growe's ruling that without Grunseth, Clark was no longer a candidate. Unexpectedly, the DFL Party had produced a friend-of-the-court brief in support of Clark. During the hearing, Supreme Court Chief Justice Peter Popovich disputed whether the party really lacked a committee that could determine its candidate. He had asked for the organization's bylaws and constitution to review before the hearing.

"Basically, we said that the party says it has no committee and that should be enough," Willis recalled. "It's highly unusual for the court to interject itself in a political party's internal workings." By a five-to-two vote, the Supreme Court ruled that Dyrstad, not Clark, would be named on the Republican ticket. With little explanation, the court backed Joan Growe's decision that without Grunseth, Clark was not part of a gubernatorial team. Justice Lawrence Yetka and Popovich dissented, arguing that the IR party was "disrespectful of the role of the judiciary" by bringing the dispute to the court at all. Nothing in the party's constitution prevented it from deciding which candidates should represent it on the ballot, Popovich wrote.

Rudy Perpich viewed the decision as a personal blow, because long-time Democrats that he had appointed to the court, like Justice A. M. "Sandy" Keith, had sided with Carlson. The decision so angered Perpich, he never spoke to Keith again.

Despite the satisfaction of the court decision, the relentless pace of the campaign was wearing on both the candidate and his supporters. Carlson's day began at 5:00 A.M. and ended after midnight. The Junkyard was open 24 hours a day, and in the evenings the campaign spread throughout the building. There were never enough phones or computers. "It was pretty rough stuff," Shaver said.

To add to the stress, the campaign had grown ugly. Early in the week before the election, the campaign got the first of four calls threatening Arne Carlson's life. Carlson and his advisors took the threats seriously. As happened in so many other areas, what the campaign needed appeared instantly. Several state patrol officers had volunteered with the campaign during their off-duty hours, stuffing envelopes and helping at the office. These officers formed a 24-hour security detail to protect Carlson and his family, with one officer remaining in their home every night.

The final days of the campaign were a blur of plane rides, speeches, and rallies. Polls showed Carlson ahead of Perpich, but not by much. On election night, the Carlson family had dinner with Carlson's old high school roommate Ted McKee and his family. During dinner, one network called the race for Carlson. "I went down and talked to the crowd about 10 o'clock," Carlson said, "but the truth is, I wasn't persuaded we had won."

So, he sat up listening to WCCO radio all night. Election returns came in slowly as election officials all over Minnesota counted by hand the 1.6 million ballots cast in the race for governor. Lars Carlson also was up, huddled in a room on the 24th floor of the Hyatt Regency Hotel in Minneapolis, analyzing the returns.

At 5:00 A.M., the phone rang and a Republican operative warned Lars Carlson that there may have been tampering with the absentee ballots in Hennepin County, the state's largest county and a Democratic stronghold. The absentee ballots had worried the Carlsons all night. Those ballots had been printed and distributed weeks before the election. More than 100,000 absentee ballots were out there and not one of them had been printed with Arne Carlson's name.

Late tracking polls showed Perpich creeping up on Carlson. Lars Carlson immediately called Hennepin County Court Administrator Jack Provo at home. Provo was ultimately responsible for preventing election fraud. Half asleep, Provo listened to Lars Carlson's concerns and promised to leave immediately for the courthouse.

At the same time, Arne Carlson phoned Marge Christianson, the county's supervisor of elections and a friend from Carlson's days representing the 12th Ward on the Minneapolis City Council. "How's it going?" he asked.

"Fine," she said. "You're ahead. In fact, you're even leading in the absentees."

Finally, Carlson believed he was governor.

CHAPTER TWO

THE IMMIGRANT'S SON

Carlson's Journey from Poverty to Politics

Arne Carlson was born in Woman's Hospital in New York City on September 24, 1934, under the name "Male" Carlson. He was the second son of Helge and Kerstin Carlson, Swedish immigrants who came to the United States during the 1920s. Carlson's parents both left Sweden as teenagers, but for vastly different reasons.

Kerstin Magnuson grew up the daughter of a prosperous merchant. Her father owned an eyeglass-and-watch-repair shop in Visby on the Island of Gotland, 200 miles off the coast of Sweden. Kerstin had an adventurous spirit and a lively personality. At 16, she borrowed money from an aunt in Illinois to come to the United States. It was the Roaring Twenties, and the United States embodied fun and excitement. Kerstin visited Michigan and Illinois, working as a domestic. Eventually, she settled in New York City, and got a job as a cook for a wealthy family at a time when Swedish cooks were in vogue. At this job, Kerstin met Helge Carlson, the family's handyman. He also left Sweden in the 1920s, but not for adventure. Helge sought refuge from poverty and a brutal home. For a time, he served in the Swedish

Army, where he was a standout boxer.

The two married in 1929, just as the Great Depression swept the country. When Kerstin was pregnant with their first child, Sten, they moved to the Bronx. The young family lived in poverty or on the brink of it throughout the Depression and the war years. The Carlsons moved constantly, even after Arne was born in 1934 and Lars in 1938. They lived in mixed neighborhoods of Jews, Italians, and other Southern Europeans. Helge and Kerstin kept alive their Swedish identity, though. Helge always believed Scandinavian products were the best. The Carlsons traveled more than an hour on Sunday mornings to attend services at the Swedish Lutheran Church in Manhattan. Still, they did not encourage their sons to speak Swedish, and they never lived in New York's Swedish enclave in Brooklyn.

Helge Carlson took jobs as a janitor, handyman, or building superintendent, often in squalid, poorly heated places. Arne Carlson watched his father stoke the furnace in one building, but he remembered being cold all winter. At one apartment, eldest brother, Sten Carlson, stood at the window and shot rats with a bow and arrow as young Arne watched. The children sometimes slept on piles of newspapers, and an old crate served as the family's kitchen table. When the boys wore holes through the bottoms of their shoes, and leather cost too much, their father repaired them with cardboard.

When Arne was about 6, the family found a nicer apartment. But the landlord would not rent to a family with three sons, so Mrs. Carlson pretended they had only two. She instructed Arne to come, each day after school, to the restaurant where she worked and wait there until it was dark. He was the quietest of the three boys and she felt she could trust him. Eventually, the landlord told her he knew she had three sons and they could stay.

Despite their poverty, the family did not feel deprived. They suffered no more than their neighbors. All of America struggled in the Depression and pulled together through the war years. If they waited in line for butter, they had fun waiting in line, Carlson remembered.

During World War II, the Carlsons lived for a time in a tarpaper shack built into a hill on Long Island Sound. The house had no kitchen and newspapers covered the dirt floor. The shack sat not far from a creek that emptied into Long Island Sound. One day, after the tide went out, Sten Carlson discovered half a canoe that had floated in with high tide. For the rest of the summer, the Carlson brothers navigated their half canoe around the creek and the sound. They swam well and loved playing around the creek. From shore, they excitedly watched the Navy PT boats doing drills out on the Sound. Sometimes, at night, they would see a fire glowing on the water's horizon. They didn't know then that German submarines waited not far from shore and sometimes sank merchant marine vessels.

The war consumed the imagination of the young Carlsons. Like other school boys, Arne Carlson could name every type of plane the military put in the air and spent free moments at school drawing planes. Helge Carlson served as an air-raid warden. Dressed in a white hat and armband, he patrolled the neighborhood at night during blackouts, scolding everyone caught with their shades up or their lights on. Relatives in Sweden were having a rough time, so the boys and their parents packed boxes of rice and other staples to send overseas. Arne eagerly read the dispatches from war correspondent Ernie Pyle in the newspaper and followed the battles closely.

The war seemed like a great adventure, but its reality also intruded on their lives. They watched the windows of nearby apartments as gold stars went up to mark the families that had lost a son. One day, a Japanese family disappeared from the neighborhood. No one knew where they went. Later, the neighbors discovered it was to an internment camp. One Sunday, while walking to church, the family watched as a battalion of black troops marched from the Armory in Manhattan to disembark for Europe.

"I'll never forget their faces," Carlson said, more than 50 years later. "They were the faces of kids who were frightened. They didn't know where they were going, and they might not come back. We always thought of the soldiers as being mature men. But I remember the faces of those 17- and 18-year-old kids. They looked pretty young to me."

ESCAPE FROM THE CITY

For a long time, Helge Carlson led a church group for boys. The group was asked if some of the boys, with assistance from the Community Service Society of New York City, would like to attend a special camp for underprivileged children run by the Choate School in Connecticut. Most of the boys did not want to leave the city. They felt comfortable there, despite the summer's heat and lack of recreation. But Sten wanted to go, and he reported to his brothers about how much fun he had had. In 1944, at age 9, Arne got his first chance to spend two weeks at St. Andrew's Camp. It was his first trip outside of a large city, and it would change his life.

The camp sat in the midst of a pasture about 10 miles from the Choate School, outside of Wallingford. The camp had a small lodge where meals were served and where stories were told nightly around the fireplace. Campers slept on cots in four discarded World War I tents. A three-holer outhouse, nicknamed the Purple Pagoda, provided the only toilet facilities. The campers swam in a pond they shared with a neighboring farmer's cows. They played baseball every day, had tent inspections, learned how to make an Army-style bed that a quarter would bounce off, and put on skits and plays at night to entertain themselves. The camp director, Choate teacher and wrestling coach Hugh "Butch" Packard, often told scary stories about "The Red Glow" that could run as fast as the wind and liked to eat little boys. As the young campers walked to their tents for bed, a red light could be seen in the distance streaking across the field. The camp counselors, who were Choate students, created The Red Glow scares to give the boys some excitement, as well as nightmares.

Gas rationing during the war prevented many field trips, but the campers always went to Choate once during a session to see the fieldhouse and visit Choate's plane-spotting station located in the tower of the science building. The campers hiked up four flights of stairs and a precarious 20-rung ladder to the tower to see where Choate watched for enemy planes.

When Arne Carlson first came to the camp, he was "physically just a couple of matchsticks stuck together," recalled one of the counselors. He stuttered, too. He made up for his slight size with tenacity and drive. Arne entered every contest. The counselors saw immediately that Arne was smart and tough.

When the counselors organized a boxing tournament, they paired Carlson against another youngster named Ronnie Lyman. Helge Carlson had taught his son to come out quick and hard in a fight, and Arne Carlson did. By the end of the first round, the other youngster looked bleary, but the counselors did not stop the fight. By the end of the second round, the other boy's head was red and starting to puff. At the end of the third round, he passed out. "He nearly died," Carlson recalled. "I never boxed again."

Funding for St. Andrew's Camp came from chapel collections taken at Choate throughout the school year. In the mid-1940s, the counselors, barely teenagers themselves, decided that they should look for students among the campers who would benefit from a Choate education. With encouragement from Hugh Packard, a scholarship was established. Packard saw something special in both Sten and Arne Carlson and pushed for them to get the scholarships. Sten began attending Choate, but in 1947 the Carlson family went back to Sweden.

Although the family had climbed out of poverty during the war, they slipped back afterward. Helge Carlson grew dissatisfied with America and wanted to leave. His wife disagreed, which created a rift between the couple that led to their divorce years later. After months of fighting and bickering over the move, Kerstin Carlson agreed to return to Sweden and left with Sten and Lars, who was 9. The family planned for her to get established in Sweden and then send for Helge and Arne. But Helge wouldn't wait and within three months sold everything the family had for his and Arne's passage to Sweden.

They could not have picked a worse time to return. The Swedish economy was awful. Helge worked at a dry cleaner and Kerstin waited tables, but wages were terrible. Their relatives treated the Carlsons badly. The strife between Helge and Kerstin continued. Helge grew more distant from the family, sometimes bitter and mean. The bickering at home never stopped. The area around Göteborg where they settled was going communist and the American boys were a target for teasing from the Swedish children. They had to learn the language fast, and Arne got in fights all the time. He also earned his only A in school so far—in English. By April 1948, the family decided to go back to America. They traveled on the *Gripsholm*, sharing the crowded ship with many war refugees.

Economically, the Carlsons sank to the bottom again, living in a rough area near Yankee Stadium. Arne had already finished the year at Public School 36 and started in the public high school. He got a job delivering the *Bronx Home News*. Sten went back to Choate and in the summer of 1949, Arne got good news. He, too, was getting a scholarship.

On his first day at Choate, Arne took a battery of tests. One two-hour exam covered grammar. He'd never heard of grammar and turned in a blank paper. Another two hours covered algebra. Another blank paper. He went back to the dormitory, expecting to be told to pack his bags and return to New York. It didn't happen, so he went to supper. For days, he expected to be kicked out at any moment. The school assigned Carlson to Long House, a dormitory presided over by a genteel Kentuckian named Vivian Jesse Barlow. Barlow taught piano and ran his dormitory like a home for wayward children. He believed in equal portions of love and discipline. Known as a stickler for rules, Barlow saw each student, no matter how old or how big, as a little boy.

Carlson struggled to keep up in his classes during his first term at Choate. New York public schools, the constant moving, and his time in Sweden had not prepared him well for the academic expectations of the nation's top prep school. Because he was often behind in class, he took to studying in the bathroom after lights out. In November, Barlow asked to speak with him. Carlson dreaded the meeting. He thought he certainly was going to be expelled.

Gently, Barlow described how one evening he had been doing a bed-check and in one room discovered only a pillow and a pile of covers. No boy. "I went in the bathroom," Barlow said, "and there I saw these two little feet. I've let you break the rules on studying for good reason. But you've done well. Your grades are good. You've been elected vice president of your class. You're the only freshman to serve on the newspaper and will likely be editor your senior year. You'll be a leader at Choate, but leaders have obligations. From now on, you don't break the rules."

Like Barlow, the other teachers at Choate maintained high standards, but enforced those standards with kindness. E. Stanley Pratt ruled Choate's drama and speech department like a despot. Pratt had a biting wit and sarcastically criticized boys who could not declaim properly. The school required every student to take Pratt's course in public speaking. During the first class meeting, the students auditioned by reciting the school prayer and song. Pratt stood at the back of the darkened theater, dressed in a black vampire cape. His criticisms shot out from the darkness, loud and scathing. During Arne Carlson's class audition, the first boy went up to the podium and broke into tears. "Sit down!" Pratt yelled. The next two did no better. Then, Arne Carlson walked up. The stutter he had from childhood still affected him. He mustered his courage and stammered out the first line of the recitation.

"Stop!" Pratt bellowed from the back. The speech master slowly walked up the aisle as the young Carlson shook in anticipation of a sarcastic dressing-down. Instead of criticizing Arne, the master put his arms around Carlson's shoulder and gently said that all of the students should calm down. "This young man," he said, "has a stutter." Pratt gathered all of the boys around him and explained what caused stuttering. The speaker's thoughts are moving too fast for his mouth to keep up. You can overcome it, Pratt said, and he promised to work with Carlson to control the stutter.

"This boy will be one of your class's best speakers," he vowed. E. Stanley Pratt kept his word. He gave Arne private coaching and taught him how to slow his mind, speak clearly, and capture an audience's imagination. As Barlow predicted, Carlson blossomed at Choate. He stood out as an athlete—wrestling on the varsity team as a 116-pound freshman, as a student, and as a leader.

"Choate was without question the most powerful force in my life," Carlson recalled. People often misinterpret why it affected him so deeply— there's a prince-and-the-pauper explanation. One day, a boy is eating turnips and potatoes in a rundown basement apartment. The next, he's dining on scallops and salad at the nation's top prep school.

"Choate was really a set of values that you took with you for the balance of your life," Carlson explained. Those values included behaving honorably, telling the truth even when it made you look bad, and working to the best of your ability. They encompassed understanding the limits that society placed on you and not expecting exceptions to those limits. Even the Socratic method of teaching used by the instructors shaped Carlson. That's where he got his sense of sarcasm, he said.

Carlson hated leaving Choate. In contrast to the uncertainty of his home life, he felt secure, happy, and challenged there. After applying to several Ivy League schools, Carlson accepted a scholarship from Williams College for admittance in the fall of 1953. It was the full ride he needed. Williams paled in comparison to Choate. The campus was wet, cold, and muddy. Carlson waited tables in Quonset huts hastily constructed during the war. He disliked the way fraternities operated, often excluding Jews. As a reporter and editor of the college newspaper, he campaigned to change the fraternity selection systems. He also interviewed Eleanor Roosevelt and John F. Kennedy, and editorially endorsed Adlai Stevenson for President. In his parting shot as editor of the campus paper, Carlson called his fellow students "mugwumps." His generation was too satisfied and too eager to go along with the status quo, he said.

The 1950s were a quiet time in politics, but the McCarthy hearings of the early 1950s taught Arne Carlson what he was against. He declared himself a Democrat.

A MOVE TO THE MIDWEST

After graduation in 1957, Carlson enrolled at the University of Minnesota in the graduate program in history. He also took a position as counselor at the Chi Psi fraternity house on campus. He made many friends among the undergraduate members of the fraternity. Carlson was a staunch Democrat in those days, and most of the undergrads favored Republicans. They liked Carlson, though, and the young men of Chi Psi later would provide vital assistance to his campaigns for public office. In 1959, he began working for Senator Hubert H. Humphrey's presidential campaign. Carlson organized voters in Wisconsin and in West Virginia. Humphrey's loss to John Kennedy angered Carlson, who felt strongly that the Kennedy family had bought the election for their son. Discouraged, he returned to Minnesota and began working in public relations, first for Control Data and then the Easter Seal Society. He also switched parties and declared himself a Republican.

In 1965, he made two radical changes in his life. He decided to run for his first political office, a seat on the Minneapolis City Council. He also married Barbara Duffy, the gregarious daughter of a wealthy lumberyard owner from Anoka. Temperamentally, Barbara was Arne's polar opposite, but they shared a love for politics and for their children. During their 12 years together, the Carlsons had three children. They lost their first daughter, Kristen, to crib death in 1966. They later adopted a son, Tucker, and had a daughter, Anne.

Carlson won election to the 12th Ward Minneapolis seat, defeating veteran Dick Franson and giving the Republicans (they were called Independents) a majority on the council. Franson challenged the election results, claiming that a piece of Carlson literature that looked like a property tax form was misleading. The literature pointed out how much taxes would be raised if Franson were elected. The case went to the Minnesota Supreme Court, which ruled in Carlson's favor.

The controversy had the unintended effect of making 33-year-old Arne Carlson an important figure in Minneapolis politics. In 1968, Carlson challenged Minneapolis Mayor Arthur Naftalin. Carlson reached out to younger Republicans, building a group of supporters that would work with him over the next 20 years. The race was close. Carlson lost by less than 2 percent of the vote and won several north-side wards, unexpected territory for a Republican.

In 1970, Carlson was elected to the legislature, representing District 36, his home ground in south Minneapolis. From the beginning, he showed a talent for debate and eventually became a floor whip. During his eight years in the legislature, Carlson earned a reputation as a "minority shark." Republicans often called on him to blast holes in Democratic arguments. Carlson's legislative seatmate, Douglas Ewald, remembered that his job was to keep Carlson's bill book on the proper page, so Carlson could be ready to lambast his opponents on whatever issue was under debate. If argument didn't work, Carlson resorted to humor. Late in his legislative career, Carlson had a favorite trick to use on legislators who talked too long. Carlson sent a message to the offending legislator via a House page. The message asked for an urgent meeting and was signed "Rudy," for then–Governor Rudy Perpich. Then Carlson and other Republicans laughed as the talkative legislator preened and set off for his imagined audience with the governor. As a Republican, Carlson earned a reputation as a moderate to liberal legislator with a strong commitment to education.

In 1978, Carlson challenged Robert Mattson for the auditor's seat. It was a raucous election leading to the Minnesota Massacre. Voters threw Democrats out of both U.S. Senate seats and the governor's office. The turning tide swept Carlson into office as well. The auditor's office had always been a quiet, green-eyeshade position. Determined to change that, Carlson first updated all of the auditor's systems. He insisted on installing word processors and other technology to make audit production less tedious, despite complaints from some in the office that computers were only a fad. He also established uniform standards in accounting practices for cities and other entities to use. He earned a reputation as a whistle blower willing to bring to light sloppy recordkeeping and mistakes made by governments.

His biggest accomplishment, a fight that Carlson said "took two years out of my life," was to reform the way Minnesota invested its state employee pension funds. As a constitutional officer, Carlson sat on the State Investment Board. He was shocked by the low returns the state was earning on its massive employee pension funds. The state had always managed its funds internally and extremely conservatively. Under pressure from Carlson, the legislature passed a law allowing the state to hire outside managers to invest its funds and to increase the percentage of state funds invested in higher-yielding stocks.

While Carlson flirted with the idea of running for governor in 1982 and made a more serious attempt in 1986, neither time felt right for him. He was married now to Susan Shepard and they had a young daughter. By 1988, supporters saw he was serious about running in 1990. The state had grown disenchanted with Rudy Perpich, who'd earned the nickname "Governor Goofy." Carlson's staff at the auditor's office noticed how often conversations led to a discussion of how he would reform education in the state and how frequently sentences began, "If I were governor."

CHAPTER THREE

"THE WORST YEAR OF MY LIFE"

What a Mess: State Faces Financial Crisis, Vetoes Miss Deadline

There's a story about the days after the inauguration of Arne Carlson as governor. One day, a transition worker went into the governor's Capitol office to check on some paperwork. He walked around behind the governor's desk and pulled out the chair to sit down.

The governor's chair collapsed in front of him. Not everyone believed the tale or the theory that the chair had been sabotaged, but "that chair was a mess," said one former aide to Carlson. The state's finances were in no better shape. Carlson's campaign predictions that the state faced a huge budget shortfall proved true. The November state revenue forecast, issued within weeks of the election, showed the state with a $197 million shortfall for the current budget period, which was to end in six months. The state would not even have enough money to complete this budget cycle without serious cuts. Worse still, the projections for the next two-year budget period showed an expected shortfall of $1.8 billion, or roughly 10 percent of the state's spending for the period. This was no surprise to Carlson, who had repeatedly told campaign audiences that the state was living well beyond its means.

Since 1973, state spending had increased an average of 22 percent per two-year budget cycle. In the previous year, state government had been spending hundreds of thousands of dollars a day more than it took in. Throughout the 1980s, the state nurtured a "culture of affluence," veteran Capitol reporter Dane Smith wrote in the *Star Tribune*. The state built beautiful new buildings for the court system and the Minnesota Historical Society, and remodeled the offices of state agencies. By 1991, the state spent 20 percent more per person than the national average, and Minnesota ranked 5th among all states in spending per capita, compared to 15th two decades earlier. The recession that began in 1990 disturbed the flow of cash into the state, and suddenly the money ran short. Dealing with this fiscal mess dominated the first year—in fact, most of the first term—of Carlson's time as governor. He did not fear the budget problems.

"I always wanted to be governor during a transition because transitions are when you can have an impact," Carlson said. "Look at FDR. He had an impact because he came in during the Depression. The good news about the budget deficit was that it allowed us to focus on the cost drivers and get at reforms. We fully intended—even as we were dealing with the budget problems—to get at welfare. We fully intended to get at workers' compensation. We fully intended to get into health care, and we wanted to get into education."

First, the new governor had to get into his office. Shortly after the election, Perpich began distancing himself from the state's financial problems. He refused to comply with Carlson's initial requests that state agencies reduce spending by limiting out-of-state travel and not completing non-essential contracts or filling nonessential positions. He even refused to allow Carlson and his wife, Susan, to tour the Governor's Residence that would be their new home.

Lars Carlson ran Carlson's transition team with help from many people, including Craig Shaver and Gregg Peterson. "There was a total lack of cooperation from Perpich's office and the legislature," said Shaver. "It's no mystery what they were doing—acting bipartisan on the little issues and then sandbagging us on everything important."

The level of distrust between the Perpich and Carlson camps ran high. Perpich refused to allow Carlson's people into the governor's Capitol suite to set up shop before the inauguration. So, the Carlson people moved in on the Sunday before the new governor's Monday swearing-in ceremony.

"My first day as an employee was the day he was sworn in," remembered Geoff Michel, a Carlson legislative liaison in 1991 and later the governor's legal counsel. "I was shown my new office and it looked like it had been ransacked. It wasn't just things out of place, but files, books, and papers on the floor."

The office computers went on the fritz immediately, and no one knew how to run the telephone system. "We just couldn't do it," said Carlson office manager Marcia Farinacci of the administration's early days. Because Perpich had been unwilling to contain spending, the new governor had only a limited budget for his staff. The Carlson staff often borrowed help from state agencies. "We could hardly buy paper," said Farinacci. "We were constantly running low on the most basic supplies."

Carlson's original staff had about a dozen fewer people than Perpich had because of the lack of resources. The office's one full-time receptionist, Mary Stibbe, sometimes fielded up to 1,000 calls a day.

Perpich ended what one columnist called "his two-month snit" by skipping Carlson's inauguration. Despite the enormity of the budget problems ahead, Carlson promised an administration that would focus on children and creating opportunities. In both his Inaugural Address and his State of the State speech later in the month, Carlson hit on themes that would become familiar over the next eight years: fiscal restraint and a "prevention agenda" to help children grow up safe and healthy. Carlson believed that as a moderate Republican who was not beholden to many special interests, he could forge consensus. He asked his transition team to seek out "the best and the brightest" to fill staff and agency positions. As communications director, he hired the press secretary to his one-time opponent, David Printy. Several

Democrats found slots in Carlson's administration. For chief of staff, he sought out Lyall Schwarzkopf, a respected administrator whom Carlson had known from his early days in Minneapolis politics.

"I want a new pragmatism," Carlson said, "where those of us in government no longer focus on the process, but rather on the substance of politics—on the consumer, on the outcome, on the people."

Three hours after he was sworn in, Carlson signed two executive orders. One established a code of ethics for his administration; the other asked agencies to curb spending as much as possible.

BUDGET BATTLES BEGIN

By mid-January, Carlson submitted his first budget, a plan to cut $194 million in spending over the next six months. Carlson resisted DFL suggestions that he dip into the state's $550 million reserves. These cuts were "infinitesimal" compared to those that would be needed to balance the 1992–93 biennial budget, he said. The legislature concurred and quickly passed the "stub year" budget. Reporters speculated that the DFL-dominated legislature wanted to solve the problem quietly because a bigger battle lay ahead.

The Democrats already had a substantial advantage going into that battle in the estimation of former Representative Bob Vanasek, a DFLer from New Prague who was Speaker of the House in 1991. "Getting elected in the manner he did left the governor unprepared for the 1991 session. When you are in a normal campaign, you have transition teams in place before the election. He couldn't do that," Vanasek said. Carlson also came in without heavy political debts. The brevity of his campaign meant that Carlson had made few promises to special interest groups. Unlike most new governors, Carlson had greater freedom to pursue reform efforts. But the short campaign also left him without a base of loyal political support. For better or worse, Carlson stood alone, and this "enabled us to take advantage of his lack of base," Vanasek said.

As Carlson and his team considered options for state spending, they tried not to create "tails"—tails, in state budget parlance, refer to spending commitments that continue to grow in future years, regardless of the state's ability to cover costs. For example, a 10 percent increase in K-12 spending one year would create a massive tail because all future percentage increases would be based on that year's higher number.

They believed that much of the state's budget problem stemmed from spending bills passed in 1989. They also wanted to make the cuts in a way that would solve as much of the problem as possible in one year. For days on end, Carlson's team and state agency leaders met in the offices of the Department of Finance, reviewing each agency's initiatives and its expenses.

"We all had Quie on our minds," said Carlson aide Peder Larson. After Governor Al Quie's election in 1978, the state was forced to make cuts in spending. "It was like, 'OK, if we have to look bad, let's do it once. Clearly if we were going to have any benefit from this, it had to be long term. We weren't going to get a short-term benefit out of it.' "

To reduce the budget by $1.8 billion, Carlson had to look at the major cost factors in state spending: education, human services, and aid the state paid to cities and counties to buy down property taxes. Taken together, these three items amounted to 85 percent of state spending. Human service spending was up because of the recession and could not be controlled significantly. Carlson also wanted to prevent unnecessary cuts in education, especially at the elementary and secondary levels. He viewed education and child-centered programs as the centerpiece of his administration.

That left local aid to government, which buys down property taxes. Under a complicated system, the state pays part of homeowners' taxes to his or her state and county through the homestead credit. Minnesota's property tax system was widely viewed as unfair and too complicated.

Carlson decided to reduce aid to cities and counties and to attempt a reform of the property tax system in the next budget. In early February, news began to leak out about what the next budget would include. By the time Carlson announced his budget on February 21, opponents were lined up and ready.

The $15.1 billion budget increased spending by 3.5 percent, the lowest increase in 20 years. The budget included $274 million in tax increases, mostly targeted at the wealthy, smokers, and drinkers. Carlson left the $550 million state reserve intact because he thought it might be needed if the Gulf War, which was in progress, continued or if the economy continued to falter.

It reduced planned increases in most state programs, although it increased spending on some early childhood programs as part of the first prevention agenda.

His budget reduced state aid to cities by 29 percent, or $639 million through a half-cent increase in the sales tax. It increased other revenues by raising tuition at state colleges and universities and holding the line on salaries for state workers as well as reducing spending on a long list of state programs.

Carlson called it a "tough budget."

"If there were any easy choices, I'd take them," the governor frequently said. "But those who came before took all the easy choices, so we're making the hard ones."

"Various pressure groups representing special interests will not like this proposal," Carlson told the legislature in his budget message. He was right. Immediately, counties, cities, school districts, university students, and other groups began organizing to protest the budget cuts, and later to protest Carlson's property tax plan.

Senate Majority Leader Roger Moe told reporters that Carlson was "giving Minnesota a Bronx cheer" with his budget. Legislators immediately took Carlson's budget on the road for hearings at which citizens would lament over how horrible the spending cuts were. Legislators organized so many hearings on the budget and state programs that Carlson's staff joked that the state needed an AWACs system to keep track of the legislators' planes. "The Democrats had a political plan and they implemented it to perfection," said Bernie Omann, a Republican legislator in 1991 who later served as Carlson's chief of staff. Carlson's relationship with the legislature deteriorated throughout March and April 1991. Legislators simply were not used to dealing with an activist governor.

"Rudy Perpich was not 'hands on' with the legislature," Vanasek recalled. "We were used to having the freedom to run things. You'd pay attention to the governor's agenda, of course. We were used to being polite and then going off on our own way and basically saying, 'We'll see you at the end of conference committees.'"

The power struggle between the legislature and Carlson never abated. Peder Larson remembered attempting to meet with the chair of a key committee. "After a while, I just made a point of going up to the chairman's office a couple of times a week and saying, 'I'm the governor's guy on this issue. Can I meet with him?'" Larson said. He never got the appointment.

Aide Bob Schroeder said, Carlson's "credibility at first was near zero because he came into office on a fluke. It made legislators mad to find out that he did have a backbone, and could be effective, and they were going to have to deal with him."

Carlson compounded his problems with the legislature first by trying too hard to reach consensus and then by lecturing lawmakers who refused to agree. He called too many press conferences, giving DFLers more opportunities to criticize his proposals. He traveled the state extensively attempting to sell an unpopular product—budget cuts and tax increases.

"If I had it to do again, I would just refuse to submit a budget," the governor said. "I'd say, 'You made this mess, you help clean it up.' Unfortunately, the game in 1991 was sack the quarterback."

The first takedown occurred when Carlson proposed a restructuring of Minnesota's property tax system as one way to improve the state's revenue stream. The property tax system had long been criticized as unfair, with some state residents paying a small percentage of the cost of providing public services through property taxes and others paying the full cost or more. The system taxed low-value homes (in 1991, those assessed at less than $68,000) at 1 percent of their value. As home values increased above $68,000, the tax rate rose to 2 percent, and above $110,000, the tax rate was 3 percent. Home values, especially in parts of the Twin Cities, had risen significantly and many homeowners with moderate incomes suddenly found themselves with high-value/high-tax property. The system largely benefited Minnesotans who lived in rural areas with lower home values. The state bought down property taxes through the homestead credit and aid to local governments so much that local units did not feel the consequences of their spending decisions.

Carlson explained the problems of state buy-downs to an audience at Anoka High School in March. "If you're going out for dinner and somebody says, 'I'll be picking up the check,' I don't know about you, but I get a little hungrier," the governor said. Carlson frequently told the story of residents of some northern Minnesota communities who paid more for cable television than for sewer, water, and schools, combined.

Carlson proposed eliminating the so-called third tier where homes were taxed at the highest rate, and raising the rate on the lowest tier to 1.2 percent. From a policy perspective, many Democrats and Republicans felt that the state needed to reform the property tax system. Politically, property taxes were a "sacred cow," said former Representative Terry Dempsey, then the minority leader in the state House.

Twice Carlson called legislative leaders together for a Tax Summit. Held in public and televised, the intent of the summits was to force some agreement from DFLers about ways to reform the system. At the end of the second summit, held on April 3, 1991, Carlson's Chief of Staff Lyall Schwarzkopf ran through a list of principles that he said the group could agree on. One by one, legislators objected that they could not agree to these principles.

Finally, Vanasek told the governor that he would agree to set a schedule for consideration of budget and tax proposals. Painstakingly, the speaker laid out the schedule of when hearings would be held and when bills would be considered and when the governor might expect something to sign or veto.

"Well, thank you for agreeing to a schedule," Carlson said, sarcastically.

A week after the summit, the House Ways and Means Committee approved a DFL plan to raise $477 million in new taxes, $201 million more than the Carlson plan. The House budget was $375 million larger than Carlson's and included $100 million more for property tax relief and an expensive plan for universal health care. DFLers wanted to spend $300 million of the state's $550 million reserve. Carlson criticized the plan because it would force the state into costly short-term borrowing and might harm its credit rating. DFLers in the Senate could not reach an agreement, however. By April 30, a frustrated Carlson told the legislature to produce a tax bill that he could sign by May 10 or risk vetoes and a special session to deal with budget issues.

While budget and tax issues dominated state politics, Carlson was in the midst of crafting a bond-and-tax package to help Northwest Airlines, which was on the brink of bankruptcy, build a new maintenance base in northern Minnesota. Helping the airline was crucial to keeping the state attractive to business, the governor thought. He was further distracted by difficulties with his cabinet appointments. One commissioner had already been forced to resign. His new and inexperienced staff still felt overwhelmed by even basic tasks, like responding to phone calls and letters from citizens.

The legislature finally passed its tax bill on May 10 on a party-line vote in both houses. The plan would raise taxes by $483 million and relied more on income taxes than Carlson wanted. Carlson vetoed it, one of 43 vetoes he would cast in his first session, more than any other governor. Sustaining those vetoes fell to Dempsey and other Republican leaders.

"I think it took a long time for some Republican legislators to realize the position we were in," Dempsey said. "We could sustain the vetoes. It took some real arm-twisting to convince some members that there was power in this. Once we established that we could sustain the vetoes, the threat of a veto became real."

The new power was a surprise to many Republicans, who were used to being a disregarded minority. Before Carlson, "if you were lucky, you got a place to sit at the committee table for a hearing," Omann said. "When Arne got elected, there was a realization that what we said mattered. When the governor was at the table, we were at the table."

For the next week, Carlson's staff and the DFLers attempted to work out a deal on taxes. At one point, it seemed no deal could be made. But the deal finally came together with an idea to give local governments the option of increasing sales taxes by 1/2 of 1 cent. The "local option" satisfied Carlson, who wanted to separate the finances of local governments from the state. The local option sales tax and increases in income taxes on higher-income families resulted in $607 million in new taxes over the next two years. Carlson also achieved his goal of keeping $400 million in the state reserve fund.

The Democrats insisted that a significant group of Republicans—33 in the House—vote for the bill. Meeting in the Governor's reception room, the House Republicans realized that being at the table meant they also would have to take some risks. Omann remembered representatives jokingly whining, "I don't want to vote for a tax increase." He was one of the 33 who took the plunge.

In its final week, the legislature also passed Carlson's incentive plan to assist Northwest Airlines and a major bill he wanted to protect wetlands. In addition, the legislature approved a DFL-backed plan to redraw congressional and legislative district lines after the 1990 census. Many in the legislature were surprised that the bill had won approval at all. Redistricting is contentious, and it usually takes two years to approve a plan. It hardly mattered, though, since the redistricting plan was heading for a veto.

In the final weeks of the session, Carlson's staff had taken to producing very specific written messages to explain each veto. "You had so many people making assumptions about what he would and would not do. The messages were to make it clear to the legislature, and to the press," said Patsy Randell, Carlson's legislative director in 1991.

Despite the contentiousness of the session, Carlson and his staff felt they had attained some goals. The budget had been balanced and none of the decisions made in the session would have long-term financial impacts. They'd helped Northwest. They'd passed the wetlands bill. They'd vetoed a health care plan that had no financing to back it up, and an unacceptable workers' compensation bill. They'd used the line-item veto extensively to trim pork from budgets, and sometimes to deliver harsh messages to legislators who had been particularly uncooperative during the session.

They thought they might finally get a chance to catch their breath.

A VETO MESS

The press conference the DFL leadership called for Friday, June 7, began with Bob Vanasek and Senate Majority Leader Roger Moe explaining the technical requirements for vetoing bills. The two leaders had earlier been told by their staffs that Carlson returned 14 veto messages after the three-day deadline. The vetoes were invalid and the bills would become law.

The reporters asked which bills were involved, and Vanasek and Moe began listing them. "The first six or seven were really innocuous bills and you could see the pens go down and the reporters stop writing," Vanasek recalled. "Then we mentioned the strike-breaker bill. That was kind of interesting."

The strike-breaker bill banned the hiring of permanent replacements during a strike and was considered a landmark bill for labor. As the press conference wound to a conclusion, Roger Moe announced there was one other bill, the redistricting plan. The pens started moving, and in a few minutes the reporters scurried away, heading toward the governor's office on the first floor. Vanasek described walking away from the press conference feeling gleeful, and a little sad for what was about to happen to Arne Carlson.

The missed veto deadline stemmed from the staff's attempt to write complete messages with each veto and from a misunderstanding about how strictly the office must adhere to deadlines. It also stemmed from disorganization, which had plagued the office throughout the session.

Patsy Randell had gone to Iowa to visit her ailing parents the weekend the veto story broke. When Schwarzkopf explained what had happened, she offered her resignation. As legislative director, she felt it was her responsibility. Schwarzkopf, and later

Carlson, rejected it. Viewing the situation as another example of partisanship, Carlson challenged the veto decision. Judge Joanne Smith of Ramsey County District Court decided the case. Carlson, represented by his old campaign attorney, Bruce Willis, argued that the vetoes had occurred before the three-day deadline and his staff had informed the authors of the bills of the vetoes by telephone. Smith rejected the argument saying that the state Constitution is "clear and unambiguous" that vetoed bills must be physically returned to the chamber from which they originated.

On August 2, the day of Smith's decision, Lyall Schwarzkopf resigned as chief of staff, and Carlson began a reorganization of his office. With assistance from Connie Levi, a former House majority leader and executive with the Minneapolis Chamber of Commerce, Carlson sought out more experienced and more politically savvy talent for his personal staff.

"He learned an awful lot in that first year," Dempsey said. "If he could handle the kind of testy situation he went through then, he could handle anything."

This was a test no one could anticipate. The veto mess embarrassed Carlson, who prided himself on being thorough and careful and knowledgeable about the workings of government. The constant battering from the DFL, and from a few members of his own party, had taken his popularity rating to 34 percent, lower than Perpich's lowest rating. He feared that in just seven months the Democrats had achieved their political goal—to make him a one-term governor.

1991 was, Carlson said, "the worst year of my life." During those long, hot days of August, he knew it was time to regroup and decide what it was he most wanted to accomplish.

CHAPTER FOUR

SETTING
THE TONE

Carlson Assembles Team to Help Implement His Agenda

When Connie Levi first took over as Governor Arne Carlson's interim chief of staff, she called the governor's staff together for a meeting in the reception room in the governor's suite. "How many of you think we're here to run the governor's office?" Levi asked the staff. Many hands went up.

"Wrong," she said. "We're here to run the state of Minnesota."

The distinction was important to Levi, whom Carlson called in August 1991 to help him reorganize his operation. Since the hectic days of the 1990 campaign, through the traumatic transition period, and into the 1991 legislative session, Carlson and his people leapt from crisis to crisis. Legislators criticized the governor's staff constantly for not communicating well and being disorganized. The media had turned the veto debacle into a symbol of incompetence. Now, the governor needed to build an operation that would sustain him and nurture his agenda over the long term. He needed people who thought in terms of running the state, not running an office.

Levi seemed the ideal person to make the changes Carlson wanted. An experienced administrator, Levi had worked as president of the Greater Minneapolis Chamber of Commerce. Before taking that job in 1988, she served four terms in the Minnesota House of Representatives. She had been majority leader when the Republicans briefly controlled the House in 1985 and 1986. As majority leader, she had been in charge of personnel issues as the Republicans reorganized the House. She shared Carlson's moderate views, and because she planned to return to business in three months, she had no agenda other than helping the embattled governor. She also understood the problems besetting him.

"For me there was a sense of deja vu when I looked at the governor's office," Levi said seven years later. "When we [Republicans] took over the House I got lots of advice and recommendations from people about who to hire. They were trying to be helpful. What we got was other people's dead wood."

"You only have to do that once to me," Levi said. Carlson, in the hurried days after the campaign, had reached out to many other Republicans for advice and suggestions on staffing his office. When Levi reviewed which staffers were handling which tasks, she quickly concluded that many people did not have the right skills or attitude for the work that they were assigned.

Some simply were unable to do the jobs they had. Others were skillful campaign operatives, but were not temperamentally suited to running government. Others had their own agendas and did not care enough about what happened to Arne Carlson.

"If there was a shortcoming the governor had at this time, it was in not understanding that there were people around him whose interest was self-interest, not an interest in his interests," Levi said. "They had hitched their wagons to his star, not because they cared about his star. They cared about their wagons."

During Levi's three months working with Carlson, she reassigned or removed several staffers from their jobs. Personnel issues were not the only problems Carlson faced.

The job of governor—as it had been constructed during his first year—did not play to his strengths.

"What was set up was a command-and-control operation," Carlson recalled, "where everything filtered through the chief of staff, and I, as governor, was used almost exclusively in an external way. I was the mouthpiece for the administration."

Consider one workplace policy instituted in that first year. Visitors to the governor's office in the state Capitol entered a small reception area staffed by a single receptionist. If a visitor went right through a door, it led to the office of the governor and his secretary. To the left, was a door leading to the offices of the governor's policy and communications staffs, the place where strategies and ideas were hashed out. During his first year, Carlson's staff urged him not to cross the line, essentially to stay away from his own staff.

"He was chafing at the bit," Levi recalled. This style of governing did not enhance Carlson's abilities. It pushed him away from policymaking and developing political strategies—his strengths. At the same time, it put him in the role of retail politician and spokesman—areas in which he felt less comfortable.

"You can implement the job of governor any number of ways," Levi said. "It's not a cookie-cutter job."

So, Carlson, with help from Levi and other advisers, restructured the job of governor. They set a new tone for how the office would function. In the next several months, Carlson hired four key people—experienced political professionals who could help him move his agenda forward. They would enhance Carlson's abilities, and compensate for him in areas in which he was less interested.

A NEW TEAM

In September 1991, Carlson announced that he had picked a new chief of staff. He chose John Riley, whom he had earlier appointed head of the state's Department of Transportation. Like Carlson, Riley was a New Yorker, born in the same South Bronx neighborhood as the governor. A lawyer by training, Riley had worked for U.S. Senator David Durenberger for four years and had headed the Federal Railroad Administration in Washington, D.C., for six years. At 44, Riley was a pragmatic political operative at the top of his game. Riley suffered from brain cancer, but believed he was in remission when he took the job with the governor.

The media loved John Riley, and often called him Minnesota's second governor. Riley could talk policy as astutely and articulately as anyone, and he gave the governor's staff much needed direction. With Levi's help, he developed a mission statement for the office, better job descriptions, and clearer lines of authority.

"I remember when John said, 'We will get health care reform in 1992,'" said Peder Larson, then a legislative aide to Carlson. "It was the first time anyone had been so focused about what we were going to do."

"Unfortunately, John's illness was much more advanced than any of us knew," Carlson said, "probably more advanced than John himself knew."

This meant the second layer of management had to be top-notch. Riley was instrumental in providing Carlson with the kind of help he needed. He suggested that Carlson hire Cyndy Brucato as press secretary. Brucato already was a familiar face to Minnesotans. She had anchored the evening news at KSTP-TV during the 1970s. She had worked with Riley as communications director for the Minnesota Department of Transportation when Riley served as commissioner. From the first moment on the job, the outspoken Brucato promised to keep Carlson in front of the cameras.

"Let's face it, pal," she said to one reporter. "Ten o'clock at night is when a lot of people get their information. I was brought in to help interpret the governor's image to everybody."

Described by her boss as "fiercely loyal" and "a fighter," Brucato became Carlson's public voice—often saying things he could not say. She also provided Carlson with an in-house sparring partner. Their vocal arguments over both policy and strategy sent more timid staffers scurrying for cover. "There were some pulls and tugs," the governor said, "but she was always a fair fighter. She won more than her share of the battles and became an important person in terms of shaping priorities. The fact is, she cared. I have unlimited admiration for her."

Riley and Carlson also hired Ed Stringer, who had returned to Minnesota after a stint in the U.S. Department of Education. Stringer had been a lawyer at Pillsbury Company, and had a breadth of experience in managing organizations. Silver-haired and patrician in manner, Stringer rose to the position of chief of staff when Riley resigned because of his illness in the fall of 1992. Riley died 18 months later.

"I understood my role very well," Stringer said. "I was to step back and be supportive of Arne. I was to make things simple and comfortable so that Arne would have the confidence that things were being taken care of at the office so that he could focus on being his best at whatever he was doing."

Under Stringer, chaos in the office diminished significantly. Stringer instituted regular cabinet meetings so agency heads could talk through ideas and initiatives with the governor. He reached out to legislators and involved Republicans more in shaping policy. "All of this was easy to do," Stringer said, "because there were a lot of good people in the administration. It was just a matter of giving them the confidence that they had a listening ear and that I had access to the governor."

For Stringer, most days as chief of staff began with a 5:30 A.M. telephone call from the governor, a notoriously early riser. The calls usually centered on a news story or a legislative issue on the horizon or a problem within the administration. The call gave the governor and Stringer a chance to brainstorm and develop strategy.

"That was a very meaningful part of my day," Carlson said. "It allowed me to be engaged directly in developing and shaping policy."

The third addition was Curt Johnson as a policy advisor. Johnson had been head of the Citizens League of Minnesota for a decade, making him perhaps the state's most visible public-policy wonk. In late 1992, Carlson elevated Johnson to a deputy-chief-of-staff role with responsibilities for working with agencies and developing policy. (Cindy Jepsen, the governor's liaison with the legislature, held the same title.) Johnson played the role of "office intellectual." With a doctorate degree in higher education and a career spent mulling over public issues, Johnson is credited with having developed the intellectual framework for many of

Carlson's policy initiatives, including health care reform.

"It was a dynamite team," Carlson said. "In Curt, we had a policy intellectual, someone who was always thinking about ideas. Ed was so humane. He had tremendous people skills and was a real peacemaker. Brucato and I—we were the ones with a fighting instinct."

Said Johnson, "The chemistry was right. Things really jelled with that group of people. We had complementary skills, and more importantly, there was an exceptional level of interpersonal trust."

The effectiveness of that team, which can be credited with solving the state's financial problems and beginning to implement Carlson's social reforms, deeply influenced how the governor operated throughout both of his terms. He realized with this group that for him to be effective he needed to feel that he was guiding policy and that competent people were implementing the details. He also realized that to work well, he needed a carefully balanced staff.

"You need to have a mix of men and women, of different age groups, of different personalities. You need a balance," the governor said. "That's why I never liked that command-and-control model. It seemed to ignore normal human relationships. The staff really does have to play a nurturing role. You need to have time for bull sessions. You need to be able to vent. Because you don't want to do that in front of the cameras."

Keeping a mix and a balance guided Carlson's staffing decisions in the years after 1992. When Stringer left for the Minnesota Supreme Court in 1994, Johnson acted as chief of staff through the 1994 election. Johnson then became head of the Metropolitan Council. Carlson chose for his next chief of staff Morrie Anderson, who had been Commissioner of Revenue since 1992.

Anderson had a thorough understanding of state and local finances, built during a quarter of a century of work with cities, counties, and the state. He oversaw the governor's final efforts to improve fiscal management and earn the AAA bond rating, and attain many crucial accomplishments including welfare reform and workers' compensation reform. "Nobody understood the budget better than Morrie," Carlson said. "In all my years working in the field of finance, I never met anyone who could match Morrie in terms of creativity and fundamental knowledge."

When Anderson left to assume the chancellorship at the Minnesota State College and University system in 1997, Carlson called on long-time political ally Bernie Omann to shepherd the final stages of his agenda through the legislature. Omann grew up in a big political family from rural Stearns County. He replaced his father, Ben, in the legislature in 1986, at the age of 22. Omann lost a race for the 7th District Congressional seat by just a few votes in 1992. After two years as assistant commissioner at the state Agriculture Department, Omann ran for Congress again. He joined Carlson's staff as a deputy chief of staff for Carlson in 1994. It was Omann who would put together the legislative coalitions to pass Carlson's education initiatives.

"What is unusual," Carlson said, "is that no one has asked the most essential question, which is 'how did you get so much legislation passed when the opposition party controlled both houses of the legislature?' The fact is, our staff was excellent at building coalitions and Bernie was the genius of the operation. He intuitively knew where legislators stood on each concern and he would masterfully build so many constituencies into one victory after another. It was like watching Eugene Ormandy conducting a symphony. He was a genius."

With Omann as chief of staff, Carlson brought in a new press secretary to replace Cyndy Brucato who left to form her own company. Jackie Renner, also a television veteran, had the same keen mind and wit as Brucato, but a gentler demeanor that suited the governor's final years in office. "She was a solid professional and fit very well into the operation," Carlson said. "We were lucky to be able to get her."

PROTECTING THE VETOES

While his staff nurtured the work of the governor, Republican legislators protected it in the trenches. Because Carlson relied on the veto to restrain spending and direct policy, he counted on Republicans in the legislature to defend those vetoes.

In the House of Representatives, that duty fell largely to

Representative Steve Sviggum, a long-time legislator from Kenyon. Sviggum replaced Representative Terry Dempsey as minority leader in 1992. Dempsey had managed to hold the Republicans together through the difficult 1991 session and Sviggum continued the trend. Sviggum often stood slightly to the right of the governor on policy, but he was squarely behind him when the governor vetoed legislation.

"The veto and our ability to sustain it was the way that we empowered each other to be players in the system," said Sviggum, who was elected in 1978 and spent many frustrating years with a DFL-controlled legislature and a DFL governor. When one party dominates the process, it becomes "an unholy situation," Sviggum said.

It was not always easy to hold the Republicans in the House together. Some disagreed with the governor on policies. Others wanted him to pay more attention to individual legislators and their agendas. Sviggum recalled a veto override vote in May 1994. Concerned because the legislature failed to submit a balanced budget, the governor had vetoed $4.6 million in a crime bill. With the 1994 elections only a few months off, some Republicans wanted to let this one go.

"I called for a caucus," Sviggum said. "I remember coming into that room and slamming the door behind me. I said, 'Our strength is with Governor Carlson. If we once crack, the Democrats will run over us like a herd of cattle.' There was some grumbling and discussion and some members spoke up and said that we had to support the governor. Then I said, 'When we leave here, I'm going to have 45 votes to sustain that veto, and I want to know the names of the 45.'"

The veto held, by a vote of 87 to 45.

After a while, the Republicans' resolve in sustaining vetoes made it less likely for the DFL leaders to attempt to override them. "I think we got to the point, after 8 or 10 failed veto overrides in the early 1990s, where the governor got really good legs. The Democrats just didn't try anymore," Sviggum said.

"I do feel that working together and empowering each other has made us players in the system," Sviggum said. "We have been players on a number of issues—workers' comp, welfare reform, education. Those things would not have happened without a Republican governor and a minority willing to back him up."

THE HOME FRONT

Arne Carlson had been around politics long enough by 1990 to understand the personal challenges faced by elected officials. "In campaigns especially, there is a real tendency by staffs to drive the candidate as hard as possible, to overschedule, to really wear the candidate out," Carlson said. "Usually it's the family that suffers."

Carlson and his wife, Susan, were determined from the beginning to live their lives as normally as possible during his governorship and to enjoy the opportunity of being governor and first lady. Unlike many previous first families, the Carlsons were a two-worker household during his time in office, especially the second term when Susan Carlson became a district court referee. They also had a young daughter, which influenced their style and interests as a first family. When their youngest daughter, Jessica, was small, they made it a policy to have at least one parent home with her in the evening.

Social events at the Governor's Residence frequently involved children. The Carlsons entertained often, and adopted a gracious but casual and welcoming style.

"The first lady really sets the tone for the administration," Governor Carlson said. He called his wife a "role model" for others and the most successful first lady of Minnesota ever in terms of influencing public policy. "She's very calm and methodical and very good at building coalitions," Carlson said. Susan Carlson focused on children throughout the governor's terms in office, first as cochair of the Action for Children Commission, and later as a district court referee and cochair of the state Task Force on Fetal Alcohol Syndrome. She also worked for other charities and was active in preserving the Governor's Residence.

Quiet and reflective, Carlson observers often described Susan Carlson as the counterweight to her more effusive husband, the balance that steadied the governor as he faced the challenges of life in the public eye.

CHAPTER FIVE

BUDGET BATTLES

Minnesota's Budget Goes from Shortfall to Surplus

"I'd rather be a good governor for four years than a weak one for eight," Governor Carlson told a group of reporters during a discussion of state financing in late 1991. Making long-term reforms in the state budgeting process was the first of several policy initiatives Carlson wanted to address in the 1990s. "The fiscal piece was always the first piece we wanted to address," he said. Many times, it seemed like the only issue for the governor.

Despite the use of $100 million from the state's budget- reserve account and the passage of the optional half-cent sales tax for use by local governments, the fiscal forecast released in November 1991 showed lower-than-expected revenues and a shortfall of $291 million for the 1992–93 budget period, which ran from July 1, 1991, to June 30, 1993.

Long-term projections were even more grim. The estimated shortfall for the 1994–95 biennium (July 1, 1993, to June 30, 1995) had grown from $363 million to $1.3 billion. That winter Carlson's Finance Commissioner John Gunyou, Chief of Staff John Riley, and Press Secretary Cyndy Brucato made a $1 bet with the governor on how large the shortfall would be in the

February forecast. Carlson and Gunyou, who guessed $540 million, split the difference with Riley, who bet $590 million. The official estimate showed a $569 million shortfall for the 1992–93 biennium, and a $1.75 billion deficit for the 1994–95 budget period.

Though the growing gap between tax receipts and state spending was largely tied to sour economic times, Gunyou said at least half the problem was attributable to irresponsible financial management in the 1980s. Specifically, Gunyou cited a 1989 property tax reform bill and a health and human services spending package with "huge tails," plans that would have a serious effect on spending in future years.

"I think the estimates were that at least $700 billion of that $1.8 billion problem [the shortfall that greeted Carlson when he took office in 1991] was attributable to them passing this tax bill two years before," said Gunyou. "I talked with Arne about that. It is what made him so adamant that we not pass anything with those kind of tails. He was just vehement about saying 'I will not leave my successor, whoever that is, in the situation I found us.'"

The initial fiscal crisis prompted two lines of action from the Carlson administration. First, Finance Department officials had to stop the bleeding and correct the immediate problem facing the state in the 1992–93 budget period. Second, they had to create, and ultimately put into place, fundamental reforms to prevent massive future budget gaps.

THE BIG PICTURE

Despite the immediate fiscal crisis facing the state, the Carlson administration, from inauguration forward, sought ways to make permanent changes in the budgeting process.

When he took office, Carlson saw three major budget problems: The state did not set aside adequate reserves; it managed its cash flow account poorly; and it increased spending without regard to the performance of the state's economy. "No organization takes in money at the same rate it puts money out. Most organizations have an eclipse. They have high revenue streams in certain months and high outflows in other months," Carlson said. "The name of the game is to figure out how you can smooth your finances out."

With those goals in mind, the governor set out to establish a reserve account which could be tapped if, over a two-year budget period, the state's financial situation didn't match the projections made when the biennial budget was passed. He also wanted to create a cash-flow account for use when revenue streams weren't in sync with spending streams. Finally, he felt it was essential that state budgeting be tied to an index, such as the growth in personal income.

The ultimate goal of improving the budgeting process, explained Carlson, was a AAA credit rating from Wall Street. "There are multiple reasons why that is significant. One is obvious, your own self-satisfaction. Another is you get lower bond rates. You will save. When you're pumping out hundreds of millions of dollars in debt, if you can save 25 basis points or 50 basis points, that has a tendency to add up to serious money," he said.

In addition, the state's good fiscal health translated directly into a positive climate for companies seeking to remain, expand, or relocate in Minnesota. "Smart businesses tend to look at a state's finances. They want security. They tend to reject a system that has wide disparities between highs and lows," he said.

But before the Carlson administration could begin the task of rebuilding the state's budget reserve and creating a cash-flow account, it had to address the massive deficit it faced at the beginning of 1992.

With the budget-reserve account down to $400 million after the 1991 session, the state not only faced a budget deficit, but a cash-flow crisis as well. When the February 1992 estimates were released, Gunyou explained that, without legislative action, the state would exhaust its cash-flow account by October of that year, and would need to borrow more than $400 million by April 1993 to meet current state and local program commitments.

Recognizing the magnitude of the budget problem, and hoping to avoid the unseemly partisan bickering that had consumed the state Capitol during the 1991 legislative session, Carlson invited leaders of both parties to work with him to solve the crisis. Carlson's goal was to get a budget that legislators considered "vote-able" in an election year and to hold the line on taxes. Instead of an increase in taxes or borrowing, the plan called for permanent reductions in base spending levels and a lower rate of spending growth. Lawmakers essentially approved the governor's plan and the legislature actually adjourned about 10 days early.

Duane Benson, then Senate Minority Leader, described Carlson as "the big winner" of the 1992 session, even though "the budget situation for the next biennium still loomed as very challenging."

Going into the 1992 session, Carlson said, "We realized we had to make some very fundamental changes [from 1991]. And one was, we had to draw a line. That's what we did. There would be no tax increases. We had already agreed that the budgets would perform to a given index—in this particular case, the index selected was growth in personal income." By those standards, 1992 was indeed a successful session.

THE NEXT CRISIS

Benson's prediction that the next budget period would be very challenging proved accurate, but certainly not prophetic. All the players recognized the challenge they would face when they returned in January 1993.

With no long-term reforms in the 1992 budget, the newly elected legislature faced a $769 million shortfall for the 1994–95 biennium when it convened in January 1993.

Consistent with its firm, no-tax-increase stance, the administration proposed a budget plan that relied heavily on a one-year pay freeze for all public employees. It was a risky move, but Carlson and his advisers felt it was the last time they would ask a single group to make a significant sacrifice to improve the state's fiscal health. "That was a turnaround," remembered Carlson's Press Secretary Cyndy Brucato, "because it proved that he was really serious about keeping taxes low."

News of the pay freeze had been leaked to *Star Tribune* reporter Bob Whearatt, who called Brucato on the morning of Christmas Eve. Brucato recalled, "I went to Arne and said, 'You know he knows.' Arne never lies, and he would never ask me to tell a lie, so I confirmed the story unofficially." It ran on the front page Christmas morning. Carlson, who regularly called aides at 6:00 A.M. to discuss news stories, honored the holiday by waiting until 8:00 A.M. to call Brucato at home. By then, Brucato's father-in-law had read the paper and pronounced the story "news to warm a Republican's heart." His response was not unusual and the pay freeze was not as politically dangerous as some advisors feared.

DFL legislators, though not supportive of the plan, offered no alternatives. "I don't remember it being a bone of contention," said state Senator Gene Merriam. "It seems to me that why it becomes attractive is, after it's been proposed by the executive branch, that provides some political cover."

Momentum for reduced spending growth could have lost steam when the official budget projection was released in March 1993 and showed that the deficit had narrowed considerably, to $163 million. But the Carlson administration was committed to making the changes it felt were necessary to create structural balance in the coming years. Now they had the opportunity.

DFL legislators lost ground during the 1993 session when a scandal involving abuse of the state's long-distance phone account broke. House Speaker Dee Long resigned in the aftermath. In addition, it became clear that the governor's resolve to veto any budget plan that included tax increases far outweighed the DFL's resolve to advance a tax hike. By the end of the session, the DFL did not have the votes to override Carlson's promised veto.

Nonetheless, the legislature finished the session by adopting a budget plan using the reserve account and shifting costs into future years, "which would have just delayed the crisis until the next year," Gunyou said.

So Gunyou prepared a comparative piece for Carlson, outlining the differences between the administration's proposal and the legislature's proposal and the impact of the respective plans on the state's fiscal health in the coming years. "We went to Arne that night and said, well, this is what we're looking at," said Gunyou. When Carlson asked for advice, Gunyou said he recommended that the governor veto the big spending bills. "We've got higher education left and health and human services," Gunyou told him.

"We had this big discussion and the political advisers are saying, 'You can't veto higher education, they'll come screaming and hollering.' And Arne, without flinching, said, 'Nope, we have to do it. We're not going to relive that first session again,'" Gunyou said. Carlson vetoed $6 billion worth of higher education and health and human services spending that night.

Gunyou reiterated to the media that the DFL plan would result in short-term borrowing to cover payroll and other expenses. Though such borrowing would result in a relatively small interest charge to the state, its impact on the state's credit rating would certainly be felt, Gunyou said. "The real issue . . . is the threat to the long-term credit rating," Gunyou told *Star Tribune* reporter Dennis McGrath. Borrowing "is viewed as a bellwether indication to the financial community as to how well you manage your money." Shortly after Carlson vetoed the two major spending bills, a deal was struck between the administration and legislative leaders. The deal gave Carlson and the legislature joint responsibility for cutting state spending if the economy stumbled and tax revenues dropped, a mechanism, it turned out, that was unnecessary. By the end of 1993, the state was firmly in the midst of an economic expansion that would last until Carlson's tenure ended.

VETO POWER

Carlson's willingness to wield the veto pen, whether on line items or entire bills, to achieve his fiscal goals, created a new atmosphere at the Capitol. Whether the state was in the midst of financial crisis or awash in black ink, as it was in later years of the administration, the governor was not reluctant to pull out the proverbial red pen and veto legislation to force the legislature to make the changes he wanted. "I never understood why governors had not used the veto more. It's a constitutional tool. It's not there to be looked at and admired. It's there to used. And I was perfectly willing to use it," he said.

The spending changes the governor often demanded were almost always misrepresented by the political opposition as cuts. "Bear in mind, we didn't slash the budgets," Carlson said. "Primarily what we did was reduce the growth. And the provider system in government assumes that growth is already theirs. They regard that as an ironclad promise."

Dee Long took a more critical view of Carlson's reliance on vetoes. "It varies with whoever the chief of staff is, but he has tended to stay above the fray. Instead of working with legislators, he has tended to come in with [veto] threats," Long said. "I think he could have accomplished the same thing with less ill feeling toward him."

Although Republican legislators sometimes criticized Carlson, privately and in the media, for his willingness to negotiate with Democrats, they stuck with him on the vetoes, often amid strong pressure from constituents. Had vetoes been overridden often in the early years, Carlson's power would have been diminished significantly. Bernie Omann, then a legislator, observed, "Carlson's vetoes really got their attention, and ultimately, their respect."

"I was just happy to have somebody veto this junk," said former Representative Gene Hugoson.

Vetoing legislation wasn't always easy for Carlson on a personal level. Gunyou recalled a discussion he had with the governor about higher education spending after a round of vetoes. "We were talking about the University. It was during the summer. I think this was the summer after that first year. It was really hot. He turned to me and said, 'How do you sleep at night?' And I said, 'Well I have this window air conditioner so it's not so bad.' He said, 'No, no, no. You don't understand. Doing the things we're doing here, how do you sleep at night?'"

Gunyou said he was surprised by Carlson's line of questioning. "Here's this guy who has a reputation as an unfeeling kind of guy. And we had this nice talk." The two discussed their mutual agreement that there was no other choice. "It's not something you can even think about because there is no other option. If we want to condemn the state to live in mediocrity, then we'll keep passing it up the way it's been done," Gunyou said.

THE HICCUPS OF 1994

Following the major vetoes of 1993, things began to look better for the state. The budget estimate released in November of that year showed the economy had picked up, revenues were growing, and they were expected to grow in the next budget period.

Under the agreement worked out at the end of the 1993 session, the additional revenues were used to boost the balance of the cash-flow and budget-reserve accounts, helping the state avoid any short-term cash-flow problems during the 1994–95 biennium.

As 1994 began, Governor Carlson's reputation as a sound financial manager was solidifying. "Few can dispute that in both substantial and symbolic ways, Carlson has restored a sense of limits and discipline to taxing and spending policy in Minnesota government," one reporter wrote.

Having restored fiscal stability, most observers expected Carlson to propose at least a modest election-year tax rebate. Pressure for a tax cut grew when the March budget estimate showed a $623 million surplus for the biennium. Carlson resisted the urge to spend what seemed like a windfall, instead proposing that a good portion of the surplus be placed in a new trust fund and earmarked for education spending in the next budget period, when projected revenues weren't expected to grow as rapidly. Ultimately, as the 1994 legislative session wrapped up, some taxpayers, including manufacturers and some homeowners, saw modest tax relief.

The big budget news items of 1994 came long after the legislative session had ended. First, in the November elections that year, a Republican majority was elected in both houses of the U.S. Congress for the first time in more than 40 years. Republicans were swept into office on the campaign promises outlined in the famous "Contract with America." Among the proposals were major changes in the funding streams that flowed from the federal government to the states. Budget officials in states across the country needed to prepare for the changes that were likely to come.

Within weeks of the historic election, Minnesota received

another piece of news with significant consequences for the state's budget. The U.S. Supreme Court ruled in early December that the state had to refund nearly $330 million to more than 225 banks and other Minnesota companies that had been illegally taxed on interest earned from federal bonds. The $270 million surplus announced by state officials in November wasn't enough to cover the settlement, but the ruling allowed the state to pay back the disputed taxes over a four-year period.

Immediately, Governor Carlson announced that taxpayers would not be asked to foot the bill. Instead, he proposed financing the refund from the state bureaucracy with a 1 percent cut in spending over each of the next four years. Legislative leaders did not oppose Carlson's suggestion.

THE GOOD YEARS

Early in the Carlson years, the governor and his staff earned a reputation as serious and committed about fixing, and reforming, the state's finances. Several Finance Department officials were even recognized nationally for their management of the state's budget.

Once the economy turned around and surpluses were seen year after year, Carlson administration officials proved they were fiscally responsible in good times as well as bad. When major budget surpluses were projected, they were quick to offer reasons the excess shouldn't be spent on permanent tax cuts or spending increases—in other words, items with big tails.

The November 1995 budget estimate showed an $824 million surplus for the 1996–97 biennium. Despite the positive outlook, the administration carefully noted that the forecast did not reflect likely changes in federal funding for key social programs, particularly Medicare and Medicaid.

When the next forecast was released and showed a slight increase in the surplus, the administration questioned the longevity of the good situation. The surplus was less than 0.4 percent of annual spending and could easily disappear with minor changes in the economy, officials warned.

The administration's commitment to fiscal discipline, even in the good years, created a new atmosphere at the Capitol. "What he's [Carlson's] done is helped institutionalize a culture of fiscal responsibility that spreads across state government and doesn't stop when he leaves office," said Minnesota State Economist Tom Stinson.

Dean Johnson, who became Senate minority leader after Benson resigned from the post in 1992, said Carlson wasn't afraid to say some things were simply out of the question. "I would hear him say, 'We can't afford it.' People would bring proposals, there would be discussions, and he would say, 'We can't afford it. We're not going to do it. Now, what's your next great idea?'"

Wayne Simoneau, the DFL chair of the House Appropriations Committee who became Carlson's commissioner of finance in 1996 agreed with Stinson. "We have institutionalized the need to have adequate reserves and discipline in spending," he said. "It would take a decade of reckless spending to screw this up."

Stinson believed the administration's success in changing the way lawmakers viewed taxing and spending was one of the key reasons Minnesota reclaimed the AAA bond rating from Standard & Poor's in July 1997, after losing it in 1981. When Standard & Poor's boosted the state's credit rating, Minnesota joined an elite club of only eight states that could boast a top rating from all three major Wall Street bond houses. It was the only state in 25 years to receive such a boost.

In addition to restoring the state's AAA bond rating, the Carlson administration also put the state in a position to provide a 20 percent one-time property tax rebate to homeowners two years in a row, and to address key issues that had rankled business taxpayers for years.

During the governor's tenure, the sales tax on replacement equipment was eliminated completely. That tax, said Jay Novak, Carlson's commissioner of trade and economic development from 1995 through 1998, was particularly cumbersome for growing companies. "If you are a printing company, your first printing press wasn't taxed," Novak said, explaining that if that same company bought a new printing press down the road, it was taxed. "The tax came at exactly the wrong time—as businesses were growing."

David Olson, president of the Minnesota Chamber of Commerce, still lamented the state's high business property taxes at the end of Carlson's tenure, but was pleased rates were going in the right direction. Commercial-industrial property tax rates were dropped significantly in 1997 and again in 1998.

Duane Benson, who left the Senate in 1994 and became executive director of the Minnesota Business Partnership, credited Carlson with advancing the property tax decreases that were passed. "Without the governor's office, the rest of us would be looking out the window whistling," he said.

A CULTURE CHANGED

In eight years, Carlson and his staff managed to turn a $1.8 billion deficit into a $2.3 billion surplus in fiscal year 1997, a $1.9 billion surplus in fiscal year 1998. They restored the state's AAA bond rating. They provided tax relief for businesses and homeowners. They shepherded the largest tax cut in state history through the legislature, a reduction of $3 billion through 2001. They built up the budget-reserve account and created and funded a cash-flow account. And they left the next administration with a projected surplus for the next biennium. But Carlson's most significant fiscal accomplishment, according to nearly every close observer of the legislative process, was his leadership in changing the culture of taxing and spending in Minnesota.

Jim Girard, who served in the legislature from 1988 until 1996, when he became Carlson's revenue commissioner, witnessed the change in attitude the governor ushered in. "There's no doubt he's leaving a state that's far better managed and in better shape financially and organizationally," Girard said. "He's changed, almost totally, the way people think about spending money in Minnesota. Legislators talk about tails and the impact of their decisions in years to come. The debate in the last couple of years has been totally on the governor's terms."

Even political adversary Roger Moe praised Carlson's efforts. "He was lucky. He hit a wave when the national economy was growing," Moe said, but added, "He was lucky, but disciplined. He kept his focus. The things he talked about didn't have a lot of pizzazz—getting the fiscal house in order, improving the credit rating—but they were good for Minnesota."

CHAPTER SIX

BUILDING
THE ECONOMY

Carlson Lays the Foundation for an Improved Business Climate

On a pleasant April night in 1998, just a couple hours before dawn, Tanja Kozicky sat on the steps of the state Capitol, bewildered and amazed by what she had just witnessed. As the legal counsel to Governor Arne Carlson, Kozicky had spent the previous 10 days working with Minnesota lawmakers and business advocates on what seemed like a certain deal—a plan to clarify the state's antifraud law. It was a good idea that would help businesses in Minnesota, especially Marvin Windows and Doors, a vital employer in northern Minnesota.

After a week of negotiation and an unusual level of consensus, the bill had passed the Senate and seemed destined for approval in the House of Representatives as well. House Minority Leader Steve Sviggum gave an impassioned speech urging members of his caucus to vote for the bill. Then, at approximately 2:00 A.M. on the final night of the session, Representative Tom Rukavina, a DFLer from Virginia, rose to speak. He reminded DFL legislators that Governor Carlson—again—had held the line against spending, including some favorite causes of liberal legislators and their supporters.

Rukavina's remarks struck a nerve with the exhausted legislators and House Speaker Phil Carruthers—who had agreed to the antifraud bill—lost control of his caucus, Kozicky recalled. "It was pure chaos," said Carlson's Chief of Staff Bernie Omann. The deal dissolved before Kozicky's eyes. The legislature suddenly adjourned, leaving a significant northern Minnesota employer facing potential disaster.

A few hours later, Kozicky and Governor Carlson discussed whether they should do more. Marvin Windows and Doors was a Warroad-based company that employed 3,300 workers and was embroiled in litigation with a supplier that had sold Marvin wood preservative. The preservative allegedly caused premature rotting in windows and doors, and replacing the windows had the potential to cost Marvin millions. The 1991 Minnesota fraud law seemed to prevent Marvin from suing its supplier. Without assistance, the company's survival was at stake, according to its president, Susan Marvin. Other companies had faced similar difficulties as a result of the antifraud law. Key legislators agreed this was a confusing law that needed revision.

The question Carlson faced that day was whether to let the antifraud bill die or to call legislators back for a special session. An argument could have been made for letting it go. The problem centered on a highly technical section of the law dealing with the economic loss doctrine. Few people understood or cared about the issue. If Marvin had to lay off workers or close down, well, that would happen long after Carlson left office. The governor had a resoundingly successful legislative session in 1998, including passage of a significant property tax relief bill for business. Why mar that success with a potentially volatile special session? After all, the governor could call lawmakers back into session, but what they did there was out of his hands.

It was not a hard call for Governor Carlson. He was unwilling to stand by when it should have been easy to help this key employer. But he didn't want to go alone on the issue. If legislators from the area requested a special session, Carlson would consider it, he said. Within two days, legislators from northern Minnesota were clamoring for a special session. The antifraud bill was too important to let die because of late-night posturing by overtired legislators.

A week later, the legislature reconvened and passed the bill it had considered earlier, as well as unrelated bills providing funding for early childhood education and economic development. Even Tom Rukavina voted "yes" on the package. The special session marked Carlson's final legislative victory for business, and it was consistent with his approach to helping business in Minnesota throughout his eight years in office.

"Our first goal was to grow quality employment. And everything else fit into it," Carlson explained, whether it was helping individual employers, selling Minnesota abroad, or working to improve the state's climate for business. "What you want to do is to focus on the word 'quality.' That's a bit more complicated [than just getting new jobs]. That means you do several things. One is, you remove some of the punishment that your system may have. Anything that's a barrier—it could be regulatory, it could be taxes, and it could come in the form of things like workers' compensation."

The result of the administration's pursuit of quality jobs? From 1991 to 1998, Minnesota saw the creation of nearly 400,000 jobs. As Carlson was winding down his second term, the state's unemployment rate hovered near 2 percent and the biggest concern on the minds of business executives was the labor shortage.

But Carlson didn't take credit for the state's job growth. "A lot of governors like to brag about how they create jobs. First of all, governors don't create jobs," he said. "However, they can take some responsibility for the climate that they do create in the state."

"IT HAD TO BE DONE"

From his first days in office, Carlson immersed himself in business issues.

Without question, Carlson's biggest effort to assist an individual company—and encourage its expansion at the same time—came early in the governor's first term when he and his staff worked with Congressman Jim Oberstar of Chisholm on a deal involving Northwest Airlines. The effort caused enormous controversy, but Carlson firmly believed that without the deal, Northwest would have gone bankrupt or would have pulled out out of Minnesota—stripping the Twin Cities of its status as a hub for one of the nation's biggest airlines. That outcome—the loss of the hub—would have done tremendous damage to the business climate in the state, Carlson said. Because of the necessity of business travel, the hub allows companies to do quick trips to other cities. Without it, the cost—and the hassle—of doing business in Minnesota increases. So, when Carlson was faced with the decision to get involved in the Northwest deal, he moved forward and didn't look back.

"To me, it was not a close call. It had to be done," Carlson said.

At Oberstar's invitation, Carlson traveled to Washington to meet the Minnesota congressional delegation shortly after the gubernatorial inauguration in January 1991. On that visit, Oberstar first approached Carlson about the Northwest Airlines situation. The airline was planning to buy a batch of new A320 planes and needed a place to service them. Oberstar had been pushing for Duluth as a location for the service center.

"If we got this project started early enough in Minnesota and demonstrated its capability, Northwest then could be in a strong position to attract maintenance from other carriers," Oberstar said.

Carlson had appointed Peter Gillette as commissioner of the Department of Trade and Economic Development. A respected banker, Gillette understood financing intuitively. He had a reputation as a skilled negotiator who could ensure the state got a good deal. Carlson and Gillette flew to northern Minnesota to discuss with Oberstar the benefits of locating the facility in Duluth. "When we came back to St. Paul, it also became apparent that the Metropolitan Airports Commission (MAC) would also like to have that maintenance facility located here in the Twin Cities," said Gillette. So the governor asked Gillette to see if he could facilitate a joint proposal. And that's what Gillette did.

During that time, Oberstar secured a commitment from

Northwest owners Al Checci and Gary Wilson to build a maintenance facility in Duluth. In turn, the congressman told the executives that state and local interests would provide assistance with the financing and construction of the facility. Despite the congressman's overtures, Northwest was still discussing its plans with other cities, trying to get the best incentive package.

When the Persian Gulf War began in early 1991 and a recession hit the airline industry—dropping passenger boardings by 50 percent and doubling fuel prices—Checci and former Vice President Walter Mondale, a Northwest board member, informed Oberstar that they had stopped discussions with other cities and planned to build a facility in Duluth. But they had been forced to dramatically curtail plans for purchasing new planes—the ones they had planned to service at the Duluth facility. Northwest Airlines and the other carriers went into a serious economic recession, driving Northwest to the brink of bankruptcy.

Now the company needed assistance just to stay in business. Explained Gillette, "Checci and Wilson needed to liquefy their assets. There were a lot of assets that were on the books—buildings, gates, simulators—those had all been bought and paid for by Northwest." The two saw an opportunity to generate cash from those assets through a sale-leaseback arrangement, Gillette said. So Northwest approached the MAC for financing through such a plan.

LEGISLATIVE AUTHORIZATION

The proposed deals—the maintenance facility in Duluth and the financial package put together by the MAC—required legislative approval. As the bill was winding its way through the legislature in 1991, Iron Range legislators tacked on a plan that would establish a jet engine facility in Chisholm.

The legislation did not call for a direct outlay from the state of Minnesota. "What the state was going to do in essence was provide a guarantee behind revenue bonds that would be issued, and revenues would be coming back from Northwest Airlines to pay those bonds down," Gillette explained.

The state stood behind those revenue bonds, but the deal also involved collateral on Northwest's part. "The only way that the state taxpayer was going to get impacted was, if the bond went into default, and the collateral was less than what it was supposed to have been, and there was a deficiency," Gillette said. A similar arrangement was constructed for the MAC piece of the deal, but in that case, Gillette explained, only metropolitan area taxpayers were involved. The legislation had to pass through eight legislative committees and required 60 percent of legislators to support it, which the committees did. However, the bill included a requirement that a joint committee within the legislature review the actual deal, Gillette said.

Senate Majority Leader Roger Moe also recognized the extraordinary move to empower the legislative commission, which he chaired. "This deal was unusual for a number of reasons. One was its size. Two, the legislature left it up to the interim commission to make the final approval," he said. "The legislature gave up its own authority."

The legislation passed in May 1991. The state and Northwest then began negotiating specifics, including how much collateral would back the state bonds. Negotiations broke down on a number of occasions, which Carlson attributed to the state's commitment to protect taxpayers.

"There were some difficult moments, but you always expect that. I'm sure a lot of the Northwest people thought we over-leveraged them," he said. "Peter Gillette drives a hard deal."

At the same time, Northwest management was negotiating with its union workforce to reduce compensation to free up cash for the company. "All of this came to a head in 1992," Oberstar recalled. "So what we had was a whole year of negotiations on the financial package from the MAC, the union negotiations with management, and bond financing to build the facility." The unions gave up $900 million in wages and benefits to keep the airline afloat.

Negotiations floundered and several Republicans criticized Carlson for going so far to help a single business.

"There were at least three major points at which it looked like it was down the drain," Oberstar said of the deal. There was one critical point in 1992, Oberstar recalled when all the parties—the legislators, the unions, Northwest, the governor's staff, and Oberstar—met at the governor's office to advance the negotiations.

Recalled Oberstar, "This thing was just sort of lumbering along, going nowhere. And finally, I looked at the governor and said, 'I think there are too many people in this room to have a useful discussion.'"

So the governor, Northwest president John Dasburg, and Oberstar retired to another room where they got to the heart of the matter. "It was a point at which Northwest was dragging their feet, and we sat down and I made a very strong pitch to Northwest to ease off on what they were asking for," Oberstar said.

Carlson then followed up saying, "Look, this is a business deal fundamentally, but it's also public policy. I've stuck my neck out a long way for you. And I don't think any governor has done anything like this for a private sector interest. And you've got to recognize this and be flexible."

Then Carlson told Dasburg, "We need a bottom line now. Not going back to your advisers, not going back to your people, but making a policy judgement here and now." The three ironed out the broad outline of what became the final deal at that meeting.

Carlson minimized the importance of his role in the negotiations, crediting the success of the deal to Oberstar, Gillette, and John Gunyou, who provided the financial analysis of the deal. "There was nobody in a better position to assess the strengths and the weaknesses of Northwest Airlines than Gillette," said Carlson who considered Gillette one of the most aggressive commissioners to serve in his administration. "And Gunyou was a superb backup because he knew state finances." As the top-ranking Democrat in the U.S. House on transportation, Oberstar brought an insider's knowledge to the discussions. "With a line-up like that, how could you lose?" Carlson asked. "The answer is, you couldn't."

The legislative commission chaired by Moe eventually finalized the deal, but the financial troubles Northwest endured in the wake of the Gulf War prompted the company to scale back its plans. The Duluth maintenance base was completed in 1996 and had plans to employ 350 mechanics, earning an average salary of $54,000, plus benefits, by 2000. The proposed jet engine repair facility in Chisholm was replaced by a reservation center that would need 604 full-time employees, earning between $19,000 and $35,000 plus benefits, by 2000.

"A BIG BLOODY BATTLE"

At the same time Carlson and Gillette were negotiating the Northwest deal, the administration also sought changes in the business environment—primarily by improving the state's workers' compensation system. State law required employers to carry private workers' comp insurance to cover medical expenses, rehabilitation, and lost wages for injured workers. The insurance companies providing this coverage were highly regulated by the state, which translated into higher costs for employers. Minnesota had the most expensive system in the region. Workers' comp had long been blamed for companies' decisions to expand into, and sometimes relocate in, other states—where rates were just a fraction of what Minnesota businesses paid.

Jay Novak became Carlson's commissioner of trade and economic development in 1995. Shortly before he left his job as editor of *Twin Cities Business Monthly* to move to Carlson's cabinet, the magazine had conducted its first "What Business Thinks" survey of Twin Cities executives. The survey found that the executives' number-one concern was high workers' comp rates.

"In fact, there had been dozens —maybe three dozen—companies in the previous three to five years who have moved to Wisconsin, and to a lesser extent to Iowa, primarily to avoid high workers' comp rates," Novak said.

Even before Carlson was elected, it was clear something had to be done. Still the politics of passing a major reform bill were dicey. Democrats risked alienating labor—an important part of their political base. Republicans resisted the reform because they were likely to be painted as pawns of business. Finally, if the legislature passed a labor-backed bill that didn't fix the system, the urgency to make further repairs would be lost.

During the late 1980s, the legislature had passed worker's comp bills on three occasions. Each time, Perpich had vetoed the bills, which many in business thought was part of a strategy by Democrats to appear to be trying to deal with workers' comp without doing anything. With Carlson in the governor's office, some business leaders felt the time at last was ripe for reform. They wanted to pass a modification of a bill approved the year earlier, according to Mahlon Schneider, then a member of the Minnesota Chamber of Commerce's executive committee and general counsel to Hormel Foods in Austin. Schneider, who had known Carlson from his days as a fraternity counselor in the late 1950s, urged the new governor to make worker's comp reform a top priority in 1991.

A proposal similar to the 1990 bill was introduced by state Senator Florian Chmielewski and then Representative Wayne Simoneau, also a Carlson ally. At the same time, business and labor tried to agree on a bill they could then present to the legislature. In late 1990, Gerald Olson, president of the Minnesota Chamber of Commerce and Bernard Brommer of the Minnesota AFL-CIO sat down to hammer out a compromise bill. A deal was struck in early 1991 that would have trimmed workers' comp rates by about 12 percent, or $110 million.

After an internal battle at the chamber, the boards of both organizations endorsed the compromise. Later the chamber reversed itself and rejected the deal, with some business analysts predicting the measure would drop rates marginally at best, and could potentially boost costs to employers. The bill was a "hoax," according to Schneider. After withdrawing its endorsement of the compromise bill, the chamber threw its support behind a Carlson-backed bill that would have cut 17 percent, or $170 million, from the system.

The legislature passed the Olson-Brommer compromise. Carlson could have signed the bill—he certainly needed a victory in 1991—and the lack of unity among business community leaders directly led to the passage of the Olson-Brommer compromise. Carlson vetoed the bill instead. "It was a real act of independence and bravery," Schneider said. The veto ended the first round of what the governor described as "a big bloody battle."

When legislators reconvened for the 1992 session, Carlson officials had regrouped and were ready to take a different approach on workers' comp. The strategy was to pass a bill that would give the commissioner of labor and industry—then John Lennes—the ability to utilize emergency rules and implement a form of managed care in the workers' comp system. The legislation, which required insurance companies to cut premiums by 16 percent, also included benefit reductions aimed at certain injured workers, dispute resolution, and insurance regulation.

As soon as Carlson signed the bill into law, he jumped on a plane and conducted news conferences in Red Wing, Winona, Worthington, and Moorhead to talk about the need for further changes in the system. Carlson told reporters that rates were 36 percent lower in Wisconsin and between 45 percent and 60 percent lower in the Dakotas.

"This bill does not make us competitive with those states," Carlson said. "This bill is a step in the right direction."

Nearly 18 months passed before the next step was taken. In 1994, a group of moderate DFL legislators worked to push another set of reforms through both the House and Senate. DFLers, especially those from border cities, were under increasing pressure to help employers.

In the Senate, action centered around a bill authored by Senator Steve Novak, a DFLer from New Brighton. Novak claimed his bill would generate an immediate 7 percent savings for employers. Analysis by the Department of Labor and Industry showed the savings to be less than 1 percent. Novak's bill was opposed by both labor and the Chamber of Commerce. During Senate floor debate, a group of conservative Democrats, who called themselves the Wood Ticks, joined with Republican senators to adopt an amendment offered by Senator John Hottinger of Mankato that turned Novak's legislation into a pro-business bill supported by the Chamber.

Novak opposed the changes and moved to end consideration

of the amended legislation. Again, the coalition of Wood Ticks and Republicans held together and rejected Novak's procedural move. Then Senate Majority Leader Roger Moe weighed in, scolding the senators for forsaking tradition by refusing Novak the opportunity to kill his own bill. On a second vote, Novak and Moe won.

Also during 1994, Republicans and moderate Democrats in the House had a workers' comp bill ready for floor consideration. But Speaker of the House Irv Anderson blocked consideration of it.

"We had enough votes, but couldn't get the bill up on the House floor," explained Representative Jim Girard, a Republican from Lynd who later became Carlson's revenue commissioner. "Irv Anderson put it in his pocket."

THE FINAL OFFENSIVE

Following the 1994 session, Girard and DFL Representative Becky Kelso of Shakopee gathered support from enough Republicans and moderate DFL legislators to challenge Anderson in his position as Speaker. "We had enough votes" to unseat Anderson, Girard said, but, instead, the coalition used its power to put pressure on the Speaker to allow consideration of a reform bill.

Early in 1995, knowing floor consideration was imminent, a group of Republican and Democratic members of both legislative bodies met in Carlson's office to discuss the reform bill.

"At that meeting we talked about strategy and he gave us the go- ahead. He told us he would sign a bill," said Girard of the governor.

Supporters of the reform effort realized the real battleground would be in the House. "The Senate was pretty well waxed," said Wayne Simoneau, who was a DFL legislator at the time and later became Carlson's finance commissioner.

Two obstacles blocked passage in the House. First, "Irv was completely, totally, from the depth of his very being, opposed to pretty much anything that business wanted," said Kelso of Anderson. Second, supporters needed to put together—and keep together— a coalition of Republicans and conservative and moderate Democrats.

Reform supporters managed to get the bill to the floor by gathering enough votes to defeat the Speaker on a procedural ruling, Kelso said.

"I think he believed there were enough members of his caucus, plus the Republicans, who would just override him," she said. "Once you've got people who are willing to do that, then the Speaker cannot control what goes to the floor. And frankly, that was the case."

"We had enough DFLers who were so determined to finally get this issue out of the way," said Kelso of the coalition that worked to pass the bill. "They had pressure in their districts to deal with workers' comp."

DRAMATIC RESULTS

The governor worked for workers' comp reform every day of that session said then–Senate Minority Leader Duane Benson. But Carlson also delegated much of the responsibility. Carlson's ability to delegate "is one of his real strengths," Benson said. "He is a bright guy. He is one of the really bright people that's been in government. And that's not an advantage oftentimes when you're an executive, because sometimes when you are bright you tend to dive into everything, because you know about everything; you understand everything."

Benson credited Gary Bastian, Carlson's labor and industry commissioner at the time, with garnering a number of key votes in the legislature. "Gary set up shop at the Capitol and we would bring legislators over there in an unending stream and he was literally like a cobbler fixing shoes. They'd sit down, and he'd talk to them, and he'd say, 'What other questions do you have?' And then we'd bring somebody else in," Benson explained.

Said Kelso, "It was by far the worst political fight that I've ever been in. Certainly without this governor, there's no way we would have gotten that through. This was a situation of something getting through the legislature with total and adamant opposition of the leaders of the majority in both houses."

The reform produced dramatic results, said Jay Novak. "In the next 30 to 36 months, we saw a decline of about 35 percent in workers' comp premiums paid by manufacturers. We went from number 1 in the country in premiums for manufacturers to number 26."

David Olson, who succeeded Gerald Olson as president of the Minnesota Chamber of Commerce in 1991, said that years after the 1995 legislation was enacted, his members had seen anywhere between a 30 percent and 60 percent reduction in workers' comp rates. "The best news for us is that our members are finally telling us that if they have plants in North Dakota, South Dakota, Iowa, and Wisconsin, that we're finally at least competitive," Olson said.

It was important to get Minnesota's rates in line with those of the surrounding states, state economist Tom Stinson said. "That was something that was going to pay off in the short term," he said. By 1998, Minnesota had seen a 6 percent jump in manufacturing jobs while the overall number for the country was down 6 percent.

In 1997 and 1998, Carlson attacked another systemic problem for business—high taxes on commercial and industrial property. For years, Minnesota held the top spot nationally in taxes on the most valuable types of business property. After workers' comp, high property taxes were considered the state's major liability in attracting and retaining businesses.

As the state's finances improved during his second term, Carlson was determined to get some property tax relief for business owners. Commercial and industrial property tax rates were over 5 percent in 1990. The problem of high property taxes often seemed "immovable and unsolvable," the chamber's Bill Blazar told reporters.

At the governor's urging, the 1997 Legislature cut the property tax rate from 4.6 percent to 4.0 percent on properties valued at over $150,000. That first cut saved businesses about $100 million in taxes. Still not satisfied, Carlson came back again in 1998, making continued commercial-industrial reductions one of his top four priorities. With a state surplus in excess of $2 billion, it was impossible for Democrats to say no.

The governor's plan to cut rates from 4.0 percent to 3.5 percent on high value properties and to cut rates from 2.7 percent to 2.45 percent on properties valued at less than $150,000 passed in April 1998. The second reduction in 13 months was expected to save businesses another $80 million. It also knocked Minnesota out of the number-one spot in property taxes.

"That is progress," said one business lobbyist.

SEEKING GROWTH OVERSEAS

While Carlson worked to improve the business climate at home through policy initiatives like reforming workers' compensation and reducing the tax burden on businesses, he also believed helping Minnesota companies break into overseas markets was important. During trips to Washington, D.C., Carlson often visited embassies of other countries, prompting some diplomats to remark that it had been a long time since they had heard directly from Minnesota officials.

"With a governor, you can open a lot of doors you can't otherwise," explained Gene Hugoson, Carlson's agriculture commissioner from 1995 through 1998, who accompanied the governor on trips to Asia and the Scandinavian countries.

For each trip the governor and his staff made, they laid out specific goals. "You've got to develop some kind of a strategic plan. If you are to go overseas, what is it, when the trip is over, you would like to have accomplished?" Carlson said.

Carlson considered overseas travel a new requirement for governors. "The days when you can criticize governors for going overseas are over," he said. "These trips are vital not only for trade but also for understanding the world economy, which directly affects the economy in your state." In his eight years, Carlson traveled to Mexico, Asia, Western Europe, the former Soviet Union, the Scandinavian countries, Australia, and New Zealand. Carlson devoted most of his trips to promoting Minnesota business and finding new business partners.

In Denmark in the summer of 1996, for example, administration officials wanted to discuss Danish pork production since the

Danes were viewed by many as the most efficient pork produc- ers in the world. And, said Hugoson, they wanted to see if there would be "an opportunity for Denmark and Minnesota to part- ner—if not immediately, down the road." As Carlson pointed out, the two economies complemented each other nicely. "In Denmark, they're extremely efficient and very small. We're the opposite. We're a little bit inefficient and we're vast. We have unlimited potential for hog production; they don't."

After leaving Denmark, Carlson and Novak joined Kjell Bergh, a Minnesota business owner with Volvo dealerships in the Twin Cities and Florida, to meet with the executive leadership at Volvo in Göteborg, Sweden—the town where Arne Carlson had gone to school for a year in the late 1940s. The visit was designed to familiarize the corporate executives with Minnesota as a potential location for a Volvo car manufacturing plant.

While both Carlson and Bergh downplayed the possibility of Volvo building a facility in Minnesota, the governor said the pur- pose of the trip was to begin forging ties with businesses in the Scandinavian countries. "What we wanted to do was open up the doors. Sadly, Minnesota, which has such a heavy Scandinavian population, has done a pathetic job of developing economic ties with Norway, Finland, Sweden, and Denmark."

The administration's trip to China in early 1998 was its most historic. Carlson was the second American governor to meet with President Jiang Zemin [the first was the Chinese-American governor of Washington], and the visit took place in the midst of the Asian financial crisis. President Jiang used the news confer- ence held after his meeting with Carlson to announce that China would not devalue its currency. The crucial announcement was carried live to viewers and listeners worldwide.

Novak, who accompanied the governor on the trip, said Carlson's performance with the Chinese leaders, particularly Jiang, was exceptional. "We were scheduled for 12- to 13-hour days and there was a 14-hour time difference. But the governor was right on target. He charmed the Chinese with his knowl- edge," said Novak.

At one point during a discussion with the Chinese foreign minister, Tang Jiaxuan, the minister said to Carlson, "We should acknowledge that there's a lot that divides us too," referring to human rights abuses and issues surrounding nuclear proliferation. There were two wrong answers to Tang's statement, Novak said, "Yes, you're right," and, "No, you're wrong." Instead, Carlson gave exactly the right answer, telling Tang, "We are interested in trade. Those are not issues that it's appropriate for us to be concerned with."

SELLING MINNESOTA

A governor's involvement isn't just valuable in courting business opportunities in overseas markets, and Carlson recognized that. He and his staff spent a good amount of time selling Minnesota to companies considering relocation or expansion.

"This is where I tend to disagree with some of the more conservative Republicans," said Carlson. "You've got to invest in the infrastructure that is helpful. It comes in several parts. One part would be direct grants, loans, and aid through the Department of Trade and Economic Development to those companies that are young. They're trying to grow, and you're trying to help them grow."

In 1995, Kevin Roberg was running a Minneapolis pharmacy benefit- management company, when the business was acquired by a bigger company called ValueRx. The parent company asked Roberg to become CEO of ValueRx, which had 11 operations in 11 different areas around the country. Roberg agreed to take the job, on the condition that he could decide where to locate the company's corporate headquarters. He seriously considered New Mexico, South Dakota, and Minnesota. "Our parent company at the time asked, 'Why Minnesota—it doesn't have a very good business climate,'" Roberg recalled, noting he thought Minnesota's reputation as a bad state for business was inaccurate.

"I talked to Jay Novak and within 10 days, we had worked out a deal where we received some funding from the state as an incentive to locate here—at the time we committed to 200 jobs. We now have 800," Roberg said in 1998. "We needed to move quickly, and one of the things I had heard was, 'You're nuts going to [the Department of Trade and] Economic Development because it will take months.' It took 10 days."

Equally important, Roberg said, was the personal sales pitch delivered by Carlson. "The governor called me and said, 'I understand that you are potentially looking at moving the company here.' Then he called the chairman of the parent company in Connecticut. And he was a good salesman," said Roberg.

Jeff Rageth, deputy commissioner of the Department of Trade and Economic Development in the mid-1990s, said Carlson was always willing to pick up the phone and make a pitch to companies. Rageth recalled a company in southwestern Minnesota that was contemplating expanding its operations and thought about moving the whole company to either Oklahoma—where it also had a facility—or South Dakota, where workers' compensation rates were dramatically lower.

"The governor called [the company president] and said, 'We really want you to stay. I will fight harder than ever on workers' comp and we'll make good on it,'" Rageth said. The state was able to offer $1 million in financial incentives, but that wasn't what sealed the deal, Rageth added. "For a governor to pick up a phone and show interest, it just means a lot."

The governor also championed Minnesota companies seeking state contracts. "Another way to [promote Minnesota companies] is to personally encourage them to bid on contracts with the state. We can't violate the law, but we can certainly be helpful. Why shouldn't a governor be pro-3M? You should be pro-whatever is in your state. I want 3M to grow and to prosper and to expand in Minnesota," Carlson said.

BUSINESS LOVES THE GOV!

Minnesotans weren't complaining about much by the time the governor wrapped up his second term in office. In fact, his job approval ratings were in the 70s, but among business executives, his support was even greater.

In January 1997, *Twin Cities Business Monthly* published the second annual "What Business Thinks" poll. The cover of the magazine exclaimed,"Business Loves the Gov!" And inside readers saw that 82 percent of the executives surveyed gave the governor high marks.

"We have a stronger economy than we otherwise would have had because he is governor," Novak said in 1998. "Regions throughout the state have benefited. Early in 1996, before the floods hit northwestern Minnesota, it was possible to say accurately that for the first time in a few decades we had no economically troubled regions of Minnesota, and no economically troubled industry," Novak said.

Perhaps one of the most important outcomes of the governor's economic growth strategy was the change it precipitated at the state Capitol. "We have been unabashedly pro–job growth, and that has translated into good politics," Carlson said.

CHAPTER SEVEN

CREATING COALITIONS

Carlson Gathers Troops for a March Down the Middle of the Road

On a cold February morning in 1993, David Leckey looked out the window of the Austin Holiday Inn and his heart sank. On the sidewalk outside the hotel where Governor Arne Carlson and his staff spent the night, protesters marched.

Carlson had hired Leckey a year earlier to build a network of supporters for Carlson's middle-of-the-road agenda. Leckey, a former public relations officer with the Department of Trade and Economic Development, held the title of director of scheduling; but his mission was to bring together groups and individuals around issues that mattered to the governor.

"It started out with the governor's sense that people were not thinking enough about where he should be and who he should speak to and why he should meet with certain groups," Leckey recalled. "It was a frustration on his part. He didn't think his time was well spent."

That morning in Austin was the second day of one of Leckey's first big coalition-building efforts—a bus tour around the state to talk about the governor's budget, especially his proposal to freeze the salaries of state employees. It would be the last big sacrifice needed to remedy the state's financial situation. The governor expected a long, bumpy ride around southern Minnesota. Still Carlson was determined to prevent legislators from taking shots at his proposals while he sat in St. Paul. The first day of the People's Budget Bus Tour had been only a modest success, with smaller crowds than expected, as well as some hostility. But Carlson also sensed support among those attending the budget meetings, and his staff urged the governor to relax and let those people express themselves.

Seeing the picketers marching outside the Austin Holiday Inn deflated Leckey. "I thought, 'Oh no, they're organized and they're going to blast us,'" he said. Then he read the homemade signs the marchers carried. "Mower County supports you on salary freeze," one read. "Please freeze teachers salaries," said another. The picketers marched for Carlson.

"It was not orchestrated by us," Leckey said. "We weren't that good at that time."

The bus trips demonstrated to Carlson that his gut feeling about Minnesotans' basic philosophy was right: People did not want a tax-and-spend government. They did want efficient and compassionate programs to deal with social problems. The trips also convinced him that pockets of support for his ideas were already out there, and that people wanted him to succeed as governor. He just needed to find new ways to reach them, ways that did not require him to go through the mainstream media.

"At that time, Arne was still very dependent on the nightly news to describe him," said Press Secretary Cyndy Brucato. "People loved it when he fought with the legislature, but otherwise they did not know who he was."

To get around that, the governor's staff made contacts with an array of Minnesota associations and organizations. The governor began to call on these groups for advice in formulating legislative ideas, and for backing once the ideas became bills. A good example was Carlson's relationship with outdoor and environmental groups. The governor had read research that showed voters were more likely to take political action based on their avocations and hobbies than they were based on economic issues. "As a public official, you could threaten people's jobs or raise their taxes and they might not do anything, but if you mess with their right to hunt or fish, look out," Carlson said. In May 1993, Carlson went to Gull Lake near Brainerd for the Governor's Fishing Opener. Despite temperatures in the 40s and snow falling on the lake, Carlson had a great time. He also came back from the opener with a new appreciation for the passion Minnesotans feel for the outdoors. He saw an opportunity to forge alliances with these outdoor people on many issues.

Associations existed for hunters, anglers, campers, recreational vehicle owners, hikers, lake-cabin owners, and other outdoor lovers. He only needed to identify and work with these groups. With help from Leckey, state agencies, and other staffers, Carlson reached out to the community of people interested in outdoor activities. This paid off when the state faced a dispute over wetlands legislation. At Carlson's request, representatives of more than 25 groups gathered for three days in January 1997 in St. Cloud to hash out the issues.

Said former Carlson Chief of Staff Morrie Anderson, "We had every viewpoint, from the radicals on one end that say, 'I have the right to drain every acre I own,' to those on the other saying, 'You should never touch nature.'" The forum gave interested parties a chance to talk together. It also gave them a stake in the outcome, and an appreciation for Carlson. Many discovered how deep Carlson's knowledge of state issues ran, and how willing he was to consider their points of view.

With support from these coalitions, the governor could exert pressure from home on many legislators. "With some of these legislators, five calls is an avalanche," said one Carlson aide.

Many of these interest groups had overlapping agendas. But those common bonds united some very uncommon groups of people, creating some strange bedfellows within Carlson's coalitions. For instance, the Minnesota Motorcycle Riders Association was involved in issues ranging from flood relief to workers' compensation reform. The 180,000-member motorcyclists' group is considered one of the most powerful associations in Minnesota because of its focus on a narrow set of issues and its ability to turn out votes.

In 1993, Bernie Omann worked as deputy commissioner at the state Agriculture Department. One day, Carlson's staff requested that Omann come to the Capitol to meet with some motorcyclists. He left his office perplexed. "I thought, 'What do they care about agriculture?' " Omann recalled. It turned out the motorcyclists had concerns about state relief efforts for the massive flooding in the largely agricultural areas of southern Minnesota, an issue that Omann handled for the Agriculture Department.

The group also got involved in workers' compensation reform, an issue that sparked an unlikely alliance between the leather-and-tattoo, Harley-riding crowd and the buttoned-down CEOs from the Minnesota Business Partnership. "It turns out a lot of motorcyclists also own motorcycle repair shops or dealerships," Leckey said. "Workers' comp was a big issue for them too."

Said Bob Illingworth, the motorcycle association's founder and executive director, "When the Carlson people asked us to get involved in workers' comp we thought about it because, while we don't like to get away from our main issues, our board decided that workers' comp was a small-business issue. A lot of our members are small-business owners. Workers' comp was killing them, and we convinced our members that the small businessperson's cost comes back to them."

Carlson, who had the nickname "Cruisin' Carlson" among riders, had a special relationship with motorcyclists, Illingworth added. "We like him. He's a different kind of governor," Illingworth said. "He can be caustic, really in your face. But he's the kind of guy motorcyclists like. 'Let's cut the crap. Let's get to the bottom line.' Carlson is a bottom-line guy."

As the coalitions developed, Carlson and his staff got better at identifying both the small issues that mattered intensely to certain groups as well as the big philosophical issues that could unite seemingly unrelated organizations. Once, Carlson met with about 150 members of the Minnesota Lakes Association for what his staff called a Fireside Chat. Held in the ornate gold and burgundy reception room in the governor's office suite, the session gave lake homeowners a chance to talk with Carlson directly. Leckey discovered before the meeting that association members wanted to know whether a small state program for voluntary water-quality testing of lakes would survive state budget cuts. When the question came up about Carlson's support for the program, he said he was familiar with it and would make sure it continued.

"Applause, applause, applause," Leckey said. "They loved the guy."

While each group had unique interests and characteristics, Carlson and his staff began to see some common philosophical issues. "Motorcyclists are every bit as adamant about their independence as deer hunters are. Philosophically, they are very similar people," Leckey said. "They want to keep government from mandating what they can and cannot do."

These independent-minded people also included many high-tech entrepreneurs, small-business owners, farmers, and others who would not always see their common interests, but shared a belief that government should be less intrusive.

Carlson's ability to pull diverse groups together was never more apparent than in the 1997 debate on tax credits and deductions for educational expenses, including private schools. The coalition supporting Carlson's school voucher plan included real estate agents, high-tech business owners, clergy and church people, and groups representing ethnic minorities, among others. About 30 organizations formed the core school-choice coalition.

"At first, many of the business groups were not willing to engage in the fight," Leckey said. "They were all involved in property taxes." The governor convinced business owners that many of their problems finding quality employees had their roots in the education system. He also promised to help bring down commercial and industrial property tax rates. As a result, education became business' number-two issue in 1997.

Carlson often said the job of translating support from voters into votes in the legislature fell to his chiefs of staff. They too knew the value of support from average Minnesotans who had an interest in particular issues.

Said Curt Johnson, Carlson's chief of staff in 1994, "The most powerful maneuver in coalition building is to get the person from below" to exert all the pressure. Carlson would use that grassroots technique to pass legislation on issues like health care, welfare reform, and the environment.

CHAPTER EIGHT

GANGING UP ON HEALTH CARE

Bipartisan Group Changes Minnesota's Health Care System

The morning of June 4, 1991, was a rude awakening for Minnesotans, many of whom ranked health care among their biggest concerns. The *St. Paul Pioneer Press* headline plastered across newsstands all over the state screamed "Health care bill vetoed by Carlson."

Furious legislators were ranting over the governor's veto of a plan to provide universal health care coverage by 1997 with a total price tag near $500 million. Representative Paul Ogren, DFL-Aitkin, called Governor Carlson a "24-karat phony with no compassion running through his veins."

"The man cannot be trusted," said Senate Majority Leader Roger Moe, DFL-Erskine.

Carlson, though, shot back. "Once again, the legislature has made a promise, but has not told the public—nor has it shared its secret with me—as to how they intend to pay the bill," Carlson said.

Although Carlson considered health care a right, he was not about to drive the state deeper into financial disarray to provide it immediately.

"The bill created a very complex regulatory scheme, and it basically didn't work," said Representative David Gruenes, IR-St. Cloud. "But that was no reason for the legislature to stop it, and, in May 1991, they gave the governor a bill that would cover all uninsured Minnesotans and make major changes in the health care system, but had no funding. The governor took a lot of criticism when he vetoed it, because throughout 1990 all the health care players, from a public-policy standpoint, were going along to get along. They left it to the governor to do the right thing."

Carlson's veto made him look like "a cruel Republican," said Anne Barry, coordinator of Human Services Funding, who went on to become health commissioner. "But vetoing that bill was absolutely the right thing to do."

Carlson considered the bill "dreadful," and another volley in a political war waged between him and the DFL-dominated legislature in 1991. Still he did not want to drop health care altogether. He felt that this would be one of the crucial issues of the 1990s; if states did not act, the federal government might act for them. He asked Health Commissioner Marlene Marschall to design the administration's response to the health care bill.

Carlson wanted a bill that would provide competition, quality care, and cost containment, and that relied on special taxes to pay for it. Under consideration were hospital and health-maintenance-organization (HMO) surcharges, tax credits, and cigarette or other "sin" taxes.

Meanwhile, Democratic legislators said they would attempt to override Governor Carlson's veto if an agreement could not be reached in the 1992 session. Paul Ogren, the volatile legislator who had been key in developing the first health care bill was "crushed and enraged" after the veto. "I think the governor wanted to be more engaged and have more of his fingerprints on it," Ogren said.

Health Commissioner Marschall marshaled her staff and legislative leaders, and during the interim between the 1991 and 1992 legislative sessions, they began to work on a health care plan that would be both accessible and affordable. "We sought out the support of the health care community and knew that not everyone would be happy, but we had to bring them to a point where compromises could be reached," Marschall said.

Deputy Health Commissioner Mary Jo O'Brien, who went on to serve as health commissioner from 1993 to 1995, was the lead person working on health care reform for the department. O'Brien worked closely with IR and DFL legislators to develop a bill that would have bipartisan support. "What was special about Governor Carlson was that he didn't try to get into the negotiations," O'Brien said. "He had trust enough in his staff to let the process go forward. He didn't micromanage, and that was an important part of the success of our efforts. He let go and let us do it."

In December 1991, after several months of meetings, a plan was presented to the governor. "It was quite well received, and from that we formed a bipartisan coalition that came to be known as the Gang of Seven," said Carlson.

The Gang of Seven represented a mixture of political ideologies, from liberal DFLers like Senator Linda Berglin of Minneapolis to more conservative Republicans like Senate Minority Leader Duane Benson of Lanesboro.

"The veto was really disappointing," Berglin recalled, "and it took several months to get to the point where I could say, 'Let's see if we can talk about it some more.' My goal was to get affordable health care for everyone, for families with children and families without children. Even though the bill was vetoed, it was a big victory, because people were taking it seriously, so the governor had to take it seriously."

In addition to Ogren, Benson, and Berglin, the gang's other members included: Senator Pat Piper, DFL-Austin; Representative Gruenes; Representative Lee Greenfield, DFL-Minneapolis; and Representative Brad Stanius, IR-White Bear Lake. Piper, who at the time was serving in the House and later went on to serve in the Senate, describes Berglin as the "workhorse."

"She did all the necessary work, but got very little press," Piper said. "Linda was the brains; Benson was superb. I think my basic role was to feed everyone; I was always bringing food."

The group needed the nourishment. They met nearly daily on the third floor of the Capitol behind closed doors to hash out the bill's provisions. "It was an improvisation on democracy," said Curt Johnson, an aide to Carlson who attended the negotiations. "Much of what happened couldn't have been pulled off if it had been open and public."

Negotiations for funding the health care plan continued through March 1992 and brought with them heated debates. Benson's office logged almost 3,000 calls during one week of the legislative session that spring. "It got pretty heated," Gruenes said. "The philosophy was that, if you keep the tax within the health care system, you contain health care spending within that profession. Some of the same groups that were saying, 'We can't be against health care for the poor,' all of a sudden were asked to be part of the solution."

Said Piper, "The eventual decision was to add a 2 percent tax to physician and dentist bills. They were horrified. I think people, nationally, were amazed that we were discussing this and were more amazed that it passed. Governor Carlson had a reputation of not working very well with the legislature; he wasn't a team player like some governors were, but, in this instance, I think he was. There were times when we thought the whole thing was dead, then it would rise out of the ashes."

The group decided to introduce the proposal as several smaller bills, rather than one large health care package. As a result, the bills could move through the legislature on a fast track, Johnson said. As the package moved from committee to committee, opposition organized. The Gang of Seven continued to meet at all hours of the day and night. Mention of a provider tax brought criticism from many in the medical community, and insurance companies brought in the "big guns," Piper said.

"We joked about them in their $3,000 suits, $200 ties, and $500 shoes sleeping on the floor of Room 15, waiting for us to hammer out details of the bill," she said. "During part of this time, I was going through chemotherapy and wore hats, because I was bald and didn't like wigs. I looked like a fat Sinead O'Connor. I kept saying, 'Do you know how much a blood transfusion costs?

Do you know how much this or that medication costs?' I was an interesting symbol of what goes on in the health care field."

The debates focused on two areas: accessibility and the rising cost of health care. "The providers wanted universal coverage, so they would get reimbursed," Benson said, "but when the tablets came down from the hill [with a provider tax], they ran for the hills."

At one point during the discussions, Benson and Ogren found themselves in a room with two or three health care providers. Emotions were running high and everyone was exhausted. "We had taken about every arrow in the Free World by this time," Benson said. "One of the providers, said, 'Would you like something to drink?' Ogren shot back, 'When this is through, we're going to be drinking your blood.' We were exhausted; it seemed like we had been wearing the same clothes for about seven months."

Lobbyists and the media objected to the meetings that were taking place behind closed doors, but, said Benson, those meetings were a necessity, allowing people to address the issues without interruption and to move ahead. Marschall agreed. "The people working on the plan needed time to work without being disturbed by misinterpretations or misunderstandings of what they were trying to do."

Later, when Benson gave a speech about the bill to the legislature, he broke into tears as he talked about a woman who couldn't afford to have a mammogram, and developed breast cancer. She and her husband lost their farm and, because the cancer wasn't detected early enough to be successfully treated, she eventually lost her life. "I was emotionally tied up in the story, but I was exhausted too," Benson said.

Discussions culminated during a meeting that ran late into the night. "The legislature was about to go into session, and we argued and negotiated through the night," said Ogren. "When the bill passed, I was absolutely euphoric. I have a poster on the wall of my family room at home that says in big, bold letters: 'Health care for all.' I had it with me in the governor's retiring room when the bill was signed into law, and everyone signed it."

A bipartisan agreement was announced in March 1992. "The governor deserves a great deal of credit for taking a very difficult position in vetoing the bill, then helping to forge a compromise," Barry said. "He became a very strong advocate of the bill."

Added Benson, "Governor Carlson empowered us to develop the bill, and he stayed out of it until the very end. He likes good performance, and he tends to delegate, which is a very strong quality."

"He could have deprived the coalition of oxygen at any time," Johnson said. "The willingness he was expressing to do it was the single greatest asset in putting the bill together. If Mary Jo and I had disappeared at any point, it would have been over."

On April 23, 1992, Carlson signed the HealthRight law, making Minnesota one of the first states to commit to controlling health care costs. "A lot of Democrats didn't like it, because it didn't go far enough, and some Republicans thought it went too far," Carlson said. The health care bill not only achieved a social goal, it also marked an important change in Carlson's relationship with the legislature. "The turning point was 1992," Carlson said. "From that point on, there was much more stability and pre-dictability, and it slowly, very steadily, started to change. I think health care was the issue that provided for that change."

Legislators, particularly members of the Gang of Seven, experienced a mixture of jubilation and exhaustion following passage of the bill. "I was thrilled," said Berglin. "It was the culmination of many years of work. The bill was harder to pass in the House than in the Senate; we didn't have any votes to spare. I went over to the House to watch the vote, then breathed a sigh of relief when it passed."

O'Brien described passage of the bill as a "great win for the governor" and the signing ceremony as a "big, bipartisan love-in."

Said Piper, "I never thought I'd see the day that Ogren and Carlson would stand together with their hands raised. This is a credit to Governor Carlson; I can't imagine the kind of pressure he got. I don't know what motivated him, but he stuck to his guns and let the people work."

A PERSONAL COMMITMENT

Arne Carlson's commitment to health care and his concern that everyone in Minnesota have access to quality health care, regardless of income, could well have had its roots in a childhood incident involving his younger brother, Lars. The Carlsons were poor and living in New York City when 3-year-old Lars developed appendicitis. Carlson's mother called an ambulance. "We were all so scared that we stood around and bawled," the governor remembered.

At the hospital, a doctor told Kerstin Carlson he would not operate on Lars until she produced several hundred dollars to pay him. Frantically, she called friends to raise money. "Lars' appendix burst that night," Carlson said, "and my mother told the doctor, 'If he dies, you will die.' There was a tremendous indifference toward poor people." The doctor did eventually operate without an up-front payment.

The HealthRight law was a modification of the Children's Health Plan, which had been established during the 1980s and provided comprehensive outpatient health care coverage for children from age 1 through 17. The new 182-page law set several goals, including cost containment, insurance reform, and state-subsidized insurance for the working poor.

Implementing the plan required "a long-term process of fine tuning and making midcourse corrections," O'Brien said. "Every year, we had to go back to the legislature with another bill to implement the plan. It was a constant process."

An important goal was to reduce soaring health care costs by eliminating administrative waste and unnecessary procedures. The law also called for the Health Care Commission to cut the growth in health care spending by 10 percent a year and to introduce competition through integrated service networks (ISNs) that would provide coverage for a fixed price per patient.

Initial funding for MinnesotaCare, the name bestowed on the new health care program, came from a 2 percent provider tax on health care providers and an increased tax on cigarettes, combined with premiums paid by people enrolled in the program.

"What the tax did was create a natural tension between the

needs and the resources," said Gruenes. "Every one of those providers paying the tax looks out for the program and makes sure the people who need it get it."

Added Carlson, "I was very adamant that the tax would stay inside the system to give it an incentive to contain costs and improve efficiency. I think that's eminently fair."

Lengthy and spirited debates evolved around the provider tax, which started out at 2 percent and a few years later was reduced to 1.5 percent because more money was raised than had originally been anticipated. "Since then, other states have tried to pass a provider tax, but haven't been able to do it," said Berglin.

Carlson also supported enrollee premiums, feeling strongly that anyone who needed medical treatment should pay something toward it. "Some people think government has to do everything for them—tie their shoes and make their breakfast in the morning," he said. "When you have a system that compels everyone to participate financially, there is less tendency to abuse it."

When MinnesotaCare was launched in October 1992, 38,000 people were eligible to enroll. The program originally covered families with children whose incomes were at or below 185 percent of the Federal Poverty Guideline (FPG) and who were not eligible for Medical Assistance or General Assistance Medical Care. In January 1993, the FPG eligibility rate was raised to 275 percent. Single adults and couples without children, whose incomes were at or below 125 percent of the FPG, were added to the program in October 1994. The FPG eligibility rate for those groups was adjusted to 135 percent in July 1996 and to 175 percent in July 1997.

Treatment options also were expanded. Initially, MinnesotaCare covered only outpatient services. In July 1993, the program added inpatient hospital benefits. Two years later, orthodontia for children was included and, in July 1996, MinnesotaCare began paying for transportation services to and from medical appointments for children and pregnant women.

By 1994, MinnesotaCare was an umbrella term for 23 programs that included requirements for simpler insurance forms, better collection of health information, and improvements in rural health care. It also addressed small business, guaranteeing employee health care coverage without underwriting restrictions. Three-hundred small businesses signed up to participate in the newly created, insurance purchasing pools.

"One provision was a guarantee that, if you left a company and decided to buy coverage, you didn't have underwriting restrictions," Gruenes said. "If you had a child with disabilities, for example, the new company couldn't say it wouldn't cover you; it had to cover you. That was another example of Minnesota being ahead of the game. The federal government passed a similar bill in the spring of 1997."

President Clinton visited Minnesota in 1994, when he was struggling to pass national health care legislation. He praised MinnesotaCare, describing it as a cutting-edge, managed-competition initiative and said it was the inspiration for his unsuccessful federal reform efforts.

By 1995, Carlson could have claimed, "MinnesotaCare is the most successful health venture in America" and few people would have disputed him.

"The reaction nationally to MinnesotaCare is still a wonder," Piper said. "I don't think I've ever been to a national meeting of legislators when I haven't been asked about MinnesotaCare."

MinnesotaCare's success has been measured in dollars and in better health. In 1993, the state asked the federal government for a waiver that would allow the state to combine MinnesotaCare and Medical Assistance, the state's Medicaid plan. Because the federal government was paying half the cost of Medicaid, the waiver would have it picking up the cost for nearly half of MinnesotaCare as well. In 1995, the federal government granted waivers to cover certain groups of enrollees, including children, pregnant women, and parents with children under age 21 whose incomes were at or below 175 percent of the FPG.

Originally operated as a fee-for-service program, MinnesotaCare in July 1996 began converting certain groups of enrollees to managed-care health plans. By January 1997, all enrollees were receiving their services through managed-care health plans. Through the program, the state had slashed the percentage of uninsured Minnesota children by 54 percent and was providing health insurance coverage for 35,000 families, 52,000 children, and 95,000 low- and moderate-income Minnesotans.

When MinnesotaCare took effect in 1992, between 11 percent and 13 percent of Minnesotans were uninsured. By 1998, that figure had dropped to between 6 percent and 8 percent.

MinnesotaCare not only improved the health care services available to low- and moderate-income Minnesotans, it reduced welfare rolls in the process. It was an effect Carlson expected, though others involved were not so sure. The governor realized that a lack of affordable health insurance discourages welfare parents from going to work because they would lose Medical Assistance. MinnesotaCare provided an opportunity to work and be insured.

By June 1997, 4,600 fewer Minnesota families were relying on welfare, saving state taxpayers $2.5 million a month. By mid-1998, Minnesota had reduced its welfare roles by 11,000 families, due in part to health care reform. Minnesota had proved that health care reform is effective welfare reform.

A HEALTHY ECONOMY

While the passage and refinement of MinnesotaCare was the major health initiative of the Carlson years, building Minnesota's health care infrastructure was another goal of the governor. The health care industry employed more than 217,000 people and contributed more than $15 billion annually to Minnesota's economy in the 1990s. Medical education and research were vital to keeping Minnesota's health care industry strong.

"The state should see itself as a partner with the University of Minnesota and the Mayo Clinic," Carlson said. "Anywhere you go in the world, everyone has heard of Coca-Cola and the Mayo Clinic. The University of Minnesota has an incredible reputation. For it to go into disrepair is not acceptable. There is no benefit to allowing either institution to decline."

When federal budget cuts threatened funding for medical training, Carlson urged the passage, in 1996, of the Medical Education and Research Costs (MERC) Trust Fund. The fund was supported by a combination of $5 million from General Revenue funds and $3.5 million from Health Care Access funds. Those funds were matched by federal monies, bringing the fund's total to approximately $18 million.

Money from MERC supported medical training for physicians, advanced-practice nurses, physicians' assistants, dentists, and pharmacists in high-tech hospitals, as well as in community clinics and physicians' offices. The fund began dispersing money to more than 300 training sites throughout the state in January 1998. In his last State of the State address, Carlson called for another $26 million to replace federal cuts in medical research and education. The legislature approved $10 million.

HEALTH INITIATIVES FOR CHILDREN, THE ELDERLY, AND THE DISABLED

Carlson was adamant that the state do all it can to take care of the health needs of children—to make sure kids in Minnesota don't have problems like his brother Lars once did in getting medical treatment.

Many of the programs the state pursued in health and education were outlined in a report done by the Action for Children Task Force, co-chaired by Susan Carlson and Ron James in 1991.

Carlson's children's agenda took a wide-ranging approach to improving children's lives, particularly poor children. For example, in 1995, the legislature passed MN ENABL (Education Now Babies Later), a teen pregnancy prevention program. Other programs pursued tobacco education for children, fetal alcohol syndrome prevention, and a special assessment program for at-risk juveniles.

The assessment program got children "an assessment of everything from their educational status to their juvenile status and possible fetal alcohol problems," said Tricia Hummel, a planner in the Department of Children, Families, and Learning. "It's a preventive and intervention program."

As a foster parent years earlier, Carlson had discovered first-hand the importance of such assessments. One of his foster children was skipping school and stealing books. "I asked him to sit down and read the newspaper," the governor said. He remembered how kids from his old neighborhood in New York would steal books if they could not read. "He was in the eighth grade and couldn't read it. I called his social worker and said I wanted him tested for dyslexia, but she couldn't get it done. I raised hell. He was tested, and it was found that he had dyslexia. You can't take away the tools that allow children to succeed. I think that, ultimately, with children, there must be equal access to opportunity, and the key is education. It's the same with health care."

The effects of alcohol on children was of particular concern to Carlson because of his wife Susan's work with fetal alcohol syndrome. In 1998, the legislature approved Carlson's proposal for a $5 million increase for a comprehensive statewide approach to preventing alcohol-related birth defects.

While Governor Carlson was an outspoken proponent for health care for children, he was equally concerned about Minnesota's aging population. In 1995, the state got federal approval to combine Medicare and Medicaid funds to establish a comprehensive range of health care services for senior citizens.

In January 1997, the Department of Human Services created Project 2030 to analyze and prepare for the impact of aging Minnesotans on several systems, including health care. Projections indicated that, as baby boomers age, the 65-plus population in Minnesota would increase to 1.2 million by the year 2030 and make up 23 percent of the state's total population. That was up from a projected 12.7 percent in the year 2000. After private individuals, the state was the largest payer for long-term care for the elderly, spending about $1 billion in 1997. That figure could quadruple by 2030.

With an aging population would come increases in people living with chronic disabilities, those needing in-home or nursing-home care, and people requiring other assistance with daily activities.

"We had to have a broad discussion about how we will care for our elders over the next 30 years and the role of government, families, and communities," said Doth. "We could no longer do business as usual."

Doth's staff met with people in the public, private, and non-profit communities to identify how those communities would have to change to meet the challenges of an aging population. "The 2030 Program has been a catalyst to get people talking about this issue," said Maria Gomez, assistant commissioner of human services. The impact would be great, affecting everything from transportation and economic development to housing and health care.

"What are we going to do when we have large numbers of 85-year-olds driving in Minnesota in the winter?" Gomez said. "Where will the labor come from? What will an aging population mean for me, for my business, for my community? We need to identify how we will meet these challenges. We have to start planning now; decisions must be made now."

Under Project 2030, the Department of Human Services began to redesign its publicly funded health and social supports for the elderly, which included new ways of linking acute and long-term care through managed-care plans. Projects such as Minnesota Senior Health Options integrated Medicare and Medicaid funding to coordinate care for low-income older Minnesotans. The Department of Human Services also began to study ways to organize, fund, and deliver health and long-term care more effectively and began moving from a cost-based reimbursement system to performance-based contracts with nursing homes that receive Medical Assistance reimbursement.

Also under the Carlson Administration, the Department of Health took a lead role in addressing health issues ranging from sexually transmitted diseases to environmental issues.

With Carlson's support, the Department of Health established a task force to study the public-policy implications of AIDS and HIV infections. The task force had the innovative requirement that at least half of its members be HIV positive. Minnesota was one of the first states to have a notification law, so that when a person tests positive for HIV, their sexual partners are informed.

Carlson also promoted efforts to help people with developmental disabilities move from institutions into the community. "A lot of the legislation to accomplish this occurred before his administration, but under his watch, almost all these people have been mainstreamed, returned to community settings," said Ogren. "The Carlson Administration pushed that reintegration, and the Department of Human Services did a lot to expedite that movement."

Added Doth, "The governor continued the process of deinstitutionalization of state hospitals and treatment centers and was behind the final push to develop alternatives. The last institution for developmentally disabled clients was to close in 1999."

WHAT A DIFFERENCE SEVEN YEARS MAKE

The headlines about health care in Minnesota could not be more different in 1998 than they were in 1991. When MinnesotaCare started in 1993, 4,932 people enrolled. By 1998, the number had risen 20 times to 102,000. The program reduced welfare costs and helped children get the health care they needed.

"It was a genuine bipartisan action," said Ogren. "A lot of people said after it passed that the sky would fall and health care costs would rise. Even with the 2 percent provider tax, health care costs have risen less than the national average. The governor's theory that this could be incorporated into the system was absolutely right. A number of other states have tried to pattern programs after MinnesotaCare, but no one has come quite this far."

The difference between Minnesota's health care reforms and those of other states was simple: Carlson and the Minnesota Legislature were willing to try a system that financed health care for low-income people by recycling money from health care providers.

"Other states didn't have governors or legislators with that kind of courage," Barry said.

"It's not a question of courage," said Carlson, "It's a question of 'why are you here?'"

CHAPTER NINE

THE NEXT STEP: WELFARE REFORM

Carlson Looks to Break the Cycle of Welfare

Governor Arne Carlson entered the ornate reception room near his office in the state Capitol on April 30, 1997, feeling proud. He was about to conduct the first bill-signing ceremony of the 1997 legislative session, and it was a bill he had been hoping to sign since he came into office six years earlier. The new law would transform the state's approach to welfare.

"This is truly an historic occasion," Carlson told the crowd. "It's an occasion when the state of Minnesota stands tall and says, 'We have a new philosophy on welfare.'"

From the beginning, Carlson wanted to change welfare in Minnesota. It should not punish people for being poor, he believed. But neither should welfare reward people for staying unemployed. Whatever welfare reform would look like, the state had to consider the needs of children first. Those were Carlson's bottom-line goals, and this new bill met each one.

"I think that the worst cruelty we can do to any human being is to say to them that we never expect them to go to work and we never expect them to amount to anything," Carlson said at the signing ceremony. "I think the greatest compassion we can extend to any person is to say, 'Yes, you need temporary help and we care about you. We're going to help you. We're going to help you get some training and we're going to help you get a job. But we also have expectations that you will do something to help yourself.'... The goal is to have children grow up in an environment where work is a way of life."

The bill Carlson signed was Minnesota's answer to the federal Personal Responsibility and Work Opportunity Reconciliation Act (PRWORA) of 1996. It replaced welfare with a requirement to work. Minnesota's legislation was modeled after the Minnesota Family Investment Program (MFIP), a pilot program in seven Minnesota counties that successfully got more than 50 percent of its enrollees off welfare and into jobs. It required parents to work or lose some of their benefits. Work was vital, Carlson said, because "we measure our self-esteem, our being, our value, if you will, in the context of what it is we do."

Before he put pen to paper, the governor had many people to thank: David Doth, the commissioner of human services who chaired a group of legislators, and other commissioners who set the groundwork for a strong proposal; the legislators themselves, who were able to avoid bipartisan bickering in their discussions; and his staff, who had dedicated themselves to supporting the construction of the legislation. But it was obvious that spring morning that what he and the rest of the crowd really wanted was to see the bill signed and sent off to Washington in time to meet an early deadline the next day that would allow Minnesota to maximize the federal contribution to state welfare funding. The documents were rushed to the office of Secretary of Health and Human Services Donna Shalala and to the department's Chicago office and, as an added precaution, faxed to the Washington office of the governor so it could be handed to Secretary Shalala in the morning. When Governor Carlson held up the final document and declared, "It is now law," the room echoed with applause.

A QUIET REVOLUTION

While the federal law finally prompted Minnesota's welfare

reform effort, the state had been quietly moving toward a welfare revolution for years. It started more than a decade earlier with a failed initiative within the Minnesota House of Representatives to cut Aid to Families with Dependent Children (AFDC) benefits by almost 30 percent. This move to reduce the primary welfare benefit program prompted the state to find ways to improve the welfare system. The Minnesota Commission on Welfare Reform — a bipartisan commission that included county officials, nonprofit providers, and advocates for the poor — studied the system during the 1980s. The commission concluded that while most welfare recipients received benefits for only a year or two, at least 10 percent of all welfare cases remained on assistance indefinitely and collected up to half of the state's AFDC payments. The very nature of AFDC discouraged work, the commission said, since recipients' benefits were reduced almost a dollar for every dollar earned by working. Subsidized child care for low-income working families wasn't readily available, making work even less attractive to single parents. The commission recommended shifting the focus of welfare in Minnesota from an income-maintenance program to a transitional program that rewarded work and enabled long-term recipients to move toward self-sufficiency.

The commission's work and discussions within the Minnesota Department of Human Services led to the development of the Minnesota Family Investment Program.

The program was created as a way to handle welfare outside of the federal system. "The fact that the people developing the proposals could step away from federal law meant that they could look differently at what we wanted to do here," said Deborah Huskins, assistant commissioner for the Department of Human Services under Carlson and an attorney in the Attorney General's office during the 1980s. "Quite early on, Minnesota adopted the position that we needed not only to get people off welfare, but also to get them out of poverty."

Getting people out of poverty, of course, is not the same thing as getting people off welfare.

"Frankly, it's quite easy to get them off [welfare]," said

Huskins. "Just cut the benefits. But you also need to get them out of poverty. The Minnesota approach was to do both."

The commission came up with what it called the "cosmic waiver." This allowed the state to seek the federal law changes and administrative waivers necessary to create the Minnesota Family Investment Program (MFIP). Unlike early welfare programs in the state, MFIP rewarded work. It required parents to support their families by going to work. Working recipients continued to receive income supplements until their income was roughly 20 percent above the federal poverty level. Subsidized child and health care made even working part time beneficial and easy. Job-placement services helped recipients make the transition to work. By combining AFDC, Family General Assistance, food stamps, and employment and training programs, MFIP streamlined the administration of the welfare program. In 1989, the state legislature approved a pilot program and the state received the necessary waivers from federal law in 1990.

NURTURING A GOOD IDEA

While the concept of MFIP germinated prior to Carlson assuming office, Carlson immediately saw the potential of this approach and encouraged the Department of Human Services to move ahead, even in times of limited resources. It took another four years to secure funds from the state legislature for the field trial, develop the details, and organize the implementation plan.

Carlson's decision to stay with MFIP was key to the state's later welfare reform, said John Petraborg, who served as an assistant commissioner for human services. "When he came into office in 1991, the state faced a very severe budget situation," Petraborg said. "Still, he made a fundamental decision in this area and, even though we were directed to find cuts in human services programs, he protected MFIP as a key to the future. That's fundamentally important. If he had shut it down, no research would have been done and there would have been no pilot program to carry forth statewide. Between 1991 and 1993, we were making some tough choices about welfare, but he always kept the focus on families and the support for work."

Huskins, who had taken two years away from the Department of Human Services to work as an attorney for the development of MinnesotaCare, returned to the department as assistant commissioner on February 22, 1994, a little more than a month before the field trial was implemented in seven counties. "My friends in health care threw me a party when I left," she remembered. "They had a cake with a woman with a briefcase and it showed her going from health care reform to welfare reform."

The cake proved prophetic. In another year, state officials could see that Congress planned to change federal welfare programs markedly. As Republicans gained control of Congress and proposals began to be presented about welfare reform, the Carlson Administration opted to take a proactive approach. Forums were held throughout the state to discuss welfare reform, health care, child care, and child welfare issues.

At the same time, MFIP was proving itself in the field. After 18 months, 52 percent of MFIP participants had moved off assistance and into jobs that could keep them above the poverty line. By supporting working families with income supplements, subsidized child and health care, and job placement programs, it seemed to be meeting its two core goals: moving families out of poverty and reducing their dependency on welfare. A report issued by the Manpower Demonstration Research Corporation, which had been hired to evaluate the field trials, supported the belief that Minnesota's project was one of the most effective efforts in the country at moving long-term, urban welfare recipients both into work and out of poverty.

FEDERAL LAW AND THE GANG OF 12

The 1996 federal welfare reform law, a multilayered, 1,200-page document, was designed to make welfare a temporary solution rather than part of a permanent problem. The law eliminated Aid to Families with Dependent Children (AFDC), which for 60 years had provided cash payments to poor families with children, and replaced it with a program called Temporary Assistance to Needy Families. This new grant combined AFDC, Emergency Assistance, and Job Opportunities and Basic Skills Training

Program into a fixed-fund grant per state. Federal dollars for public assistance, which had previously covered about 54 percent of Minnesota's needs and had increased as the welfare rolls increased, were set at a lump-sum appropriation. Those grants would not increase if the number of recipients increased. Minnesota's grant for the following six years would be $268 million, based on the state's 1994 spending levels.

The federal law required that participants work to be eligible for public benefits, and required states to enforce that rule. To avoid losing federal dollars, states had to move up to 25 percent of recipients into work or training and educational activities by 1997; by 2002, 50 percent of the caseload would have to be working or getting training. Federal law also placed a 60-month lifetime limit on the time parents could receive public assistance (although 20 percent of the caseload could be exempted for hardships), and it reduced benefits to legal immigrants who are not U.S. citizens.

Although the federal law gave states some latitude in implementing the new guidelines, it also included strict mandates. The 60-month lifetime limit, for example, was only flexible to the degree that states could shorten it. The requirement that an ever-increasing percentage of the caseload be working was a challenge all states faced.

MFIP answered most of those challenges and the state chose to modify the program to take it statewide. To do that, Carlson suggested that the Department of Human Services direct another bipartisan commission that would discuss welfare.

"We didn't start out with widespread conservative support," he remembered a year after the signing. "The conservatives wanted to go in one direction and the liberals wanted to go in another. So we had to craft a middle ground."

To do that, he put the proceedings in the hands of someone he trusted to work with the legislature, someone he knew could keep the issues, not the politics, at the forefront. That someone was David Doth, whom Carlson persuaded to come back from the private sector and become the commissioner of human services in the spring of 1996. Carlson proposed that a "discussion group" be set up to tackle welfare reform. The group would be composed of people appointed from each house of the legislature and each party. They would then work with his staff and the Department of Human Services to develop Minnesota's proposal.

"From the beginning, he wanted it to be bipartisan," Huskins remembered. "The strength of the Minnesota approach is that it has been bipartisan all along."

The group eventually included 12 legislators, half DFLers and half Republicans, as well as representatives from the governor's staff and key state departments. Interestingly, it included several legislators who had been part of the so-called Gang of Seven that had crafted the state's health care law in 1992. Representative Lee Greenfield, DFL-Minneapolis, and Senators Linda Berglin, DFL-Minneapolis, and Pat Piper, DFL-Austin, were members of both gangs.

In December 1996, that informal group began meeting two or three times a week for several hours. Doth convened and facilitated the meetings and made much of his staff available for the discussions. R. Jane Brown, the commissioner of the Department of Economic Security, cleared her schedule to attend, as did commissioners from both planning and finance.

"We'd start at about 4:30 in the afternoon and end at about 8:30 or 9:00," said Senator Sheila Kiscaden, IR-Rochester. "For some meetings, someone would bring in sandwiches and we'd just meet straight through. We'd grab a sandwich and just keep working."

"I thought it was a brilliant idea," said Senator Dan Stevens, IR-Mora, of the discussion group. "It gave all of us a chance to put forth ideas and to talk freely and openly. We didn't have to cut a deal that the rest of the legislature had to follow. We truly explored all the issues and all the options. We learned to agree on what we could and agree to disagree on other issues."

The work was both frustrating and rewarding. There were huge issues to discuss: What the grant amount would be, for example, and how stringent to make the sanctions for people who failed to comply with the work requirements. But there was a surprising attitude of cooperation in that crowded room on the third floor of the Centennial Office Building. It stemmed partly from the sense that they had no time to waste. The federal law demanded a response. The cooperation also flourished because legislators from both political parties felt some ownership of the ideas.

"We just laid it on the table—that we need to do this fast and we can't pussyfoot around issues," Huskins said. "We had to be able to lay options on the table and be able to discuss the merits and demerits of each. Everybody had to be able to feel safe in saying things without coming across in a personal way. We just didn't have time for that, and everybody agreed. We were able to establish a trusting working relationship."

Carlson was not surprised at how well the Gang of 12 and his administration were able to work together.

"When you have an enduring problem and you get people together for an extended period of time, they develop a camaraderie that is extraordinarily healthy," Carlson said. "Ultimately, it builds a factor of trust. It also allows members of the committee to begin to understand the totality of the legislation and therefore all the pieces of it. There's a lot of give and take. It's not a question of a Republican or a Democratic approach. It's a focus on a philosophy and how we continue the journey toward that philosophy."

Such a relationship was essential to the discussion. "It was difficult to deal with the 'turf' issues between different entities and the fear of the unknown by those entities and recipients," said Representative Kevin Goodno, IR-Moorhead. "The biggest challenge was getting a handle on the enormity of the task. Redesigning Minnesota's welfare system touched on every aspect of state government."

Those discussions were going on at the same time as legislative hearings on welfare reform—which proved to be a blessing for the Gang of 12. "Having those hearings at the same time allowed us to take the information that was being presented and then apply it in context," Senator Kiscaden said. "We could discuss the issues in the context of what we had heard that day. It was integrated in a way that was unusual—there were two to four hours of hearings a day, and then we'd be meeting for two to four hours in the evening about them."

The approach made the whole process slightly less painful. Although there were still vehement disagreements and heated debates, the legislature accepted the final proposal with open arms. The welfare reform bill —presented by Loren Jennings, DFL-Harris, in the House, and by Dan Stevens in the Senate— passed with almost no opposition.

"I think the fact that we did our job was proved by the fact that our welfare reform legislation passed," Senator Stevens said. "We did our work, and that's a great feeling. I'm quite proud of what happened. I think that this is one of the most important pieces of legislation passed in recent times."

A NEW PHILOSOPHY

The new law embodied Carlson's attitude toward work as well as his passion for giving children every chance they deserve.

"I'm most proud of the philosophy," he said. "It would have been reasonably normal to get caught up in the rhetoric of the debate, but we held to our philosophy. . . The question that we had to answer was, do we want those kids to grow up on welfare? The answer was no. We had to break the cycle of poverty."

"The governor has always suggested that work in and of itself, as well as work with a career possibility, is something everyone should have," said Human Services Commissioner Doth. "The strongest element of this program is that it has its incentives pointed in the right direction. It supports work. People are better off when they go to work."

The new law required parents in two-parent families to begin working immediately and gave single-parent families a six-month window to find employment. Families could continue to receive an income supplement until their income reached 20 percent above the federal poverty level (in 1995, poverty level for a family of four was $15,550). Parents who failed to go to work or to follow through with other activities to support their families, however, would see a reduction in benefits.

The responsibility for helping recipients find work fell to Minnesota's counties. The law directed counties to offer employment and training services either through two service providers or through the Minnesota Department of Economic Security's Workforce Center system, a state and local partnership that brought together state, county, and private non-profit employment and training services in one building. All 87 of the state's counties had elected to work with the Department of Economic Security and create Workforce Centers, although many would offer another service provider as well.

The legislation also provided substantial increases in state funding for child care and guaranteed that families on public assistance would have access to subsidized day care. Low-income working families not on welfare would also be assisted by the Basic Sliding Fee program, which helped pay for child-care costs. Governor Carlson, who authored the state's first daycare bill while a member of the Minnesota House of Representatives, increased the child-care coffers by more than $90 million in 1997 and approved nearly $96 million for the 1998–99 biennium.

MinnesotaCare, the statewide health care reform that was enacted in 1992 to make quality health care available to all Minnesotans and to dissuade families from going on welfare just to receive state-funded Medical Assistance, also made work more attractive to families. It allowed them to take part-time or seasonal jobs that didn't offer medical benefits without worrying about their families' health.

"We never had expectations that we would be able to get everybody off welfare," Carlson said. "It's silly to run around with this ideology that everybody is going to become independent. But what you really need to focus on is what you want to correct, which is the children growing up in an environment where there is no work. That's what this was about. It was about the child, and about making parents part of the solution."

A YEAR LATER

Has welfare reform worked?

The hard numbers say "yes." More than 11,000 Minnesotans moved off welfare by mid-1998. In addition, the reforms in health care and welfare together saved the state an estimated $200 million.

Those on the front lines say "yes" as well. Liz Victor-Flind, a Ramsey County financial worker who had worked with welfare recipients for more than a decade, saw the results every day.

"I worked with AFDC for long enough to know it was the most enabling program out there. There was no incentive to be responsible and there was no disincentive to being irresponsible," she said.

MFIP reversed that. While some recipients complained about the work requirements, most people "never wanted to be here and be on welfare," Victor-Flind said. Those clients loved MFIP. Victor-Flind remembered one man with a large family and a history of welfare dependency. For years, he had avoided working so he wouldn't lose the benefits his family depended on. "I knew he never wanted to be on welfare," she said. "He wanted to support his family himself, but he couldn't. And so, to get welfare, he had to be pathetic."

Under the new law, work became a viable option. "He called me and said he was going to be working full time," Victor-Flind said. "I said, 'That's wonderful!' I used to have to say, 'Well, sorry, but there go your benefits.'" When he questioned her about how long he could work and how much overtime he could put in, Victor-Flind gleefully informed him that he wouldn't be punished for putting in extra hours, that in fact he would continue receiving state assistance until he was far enough above poverty to support his family without aid.

Many people appreciated the new system. Jerry Vitzhum directed the Anoka County Job Training Center, part of the county's huge and impressive Workforce Center. Many of the 140 clients they served each week came in reluctant and apprehensive about the task in front of them. "They're a little antsy coming in because there's never been this requirement before," Vitzhum said of the work-preparation program recipients must go through. The two-week program identified skills and helped recipients prepare for job interviews and going back to work. "Then they start the two-week program that most people go through, and, by the second or third day, they're very much engaged in looking for work. By then they've seen that there's hope, that they will find work," Vitzhum said.

They also realized that they were not alone. All of the state's 55 Workforce Centers were outfitted with resource centers designed to help people find work. Besides having computers available to produce cover letters and resumes, there were also terminals linked to both the Internet and JobNet, which provided job listings from across the state. There were business directories, manufacturing guides, and dossiers about specific companies. When someone was ready to send out a resume or application, they could use a free fax machine to transmit the information.

The economy deserved a portion of the credit for the initial success of Minnesota's welfare reform. Minnesota's economy caught fire at just the right time, and, with an unemployment rate hovering around 3 percent, employers needed job seekers just as much as MFIP participants needed jobs. "We have an incredible economy right now," Commissioner Brown said. "Employers need people and are willing to train them."

The complete results of welfare reform would not be clear until several years after Carlson's term ended. One of the major concerns for many people involved in welfare was what would happen after the first 60 months, when the lifetime limit ran out for many recipients. These people might be the hardest to help. "That's a big issue for the future," said Huskins.

Liz Victor-Flind, the Ramsey County financial worker, meanwhile, shook her head about the people who hadn't taken the 60-month limit seriously.

"I do my best in interviews with clients to say that 60 months isn't a long time," she said. "But I'm worried that some of them don't take it seriously. As far as I'm concerned, though, they've been warned. A lot of these folks who come into my office have parents and grandparents who were on assistance. They're people who have never really known anyone who's had to work. Somewhere along the way, we have to break the cycle."

With welfare reform, Minnesota took that step.

CHAPTER TEN

A NEW DEFINITION OF GREEN

Carlson Puts Environmental Issues on a Fast Track

You didn't catch Arne Carlson on the cover of *Time* magazine, resplendent in red plaid and hoisting a prize walleye in one fist. In eight fishing openers, the governor caught only two fish—and the media often only credit him with the last one, a puny sauger out of the Mississippi River near Red Wing in 1998. Yet Carlson may have been one of the greenest chief executives in Minnesota history.

Under his guidance, the state passed the toughest wetland protection law in the country. He made a long-term commitment to cleaning up the Minnesota River, an action that led to significantly reduced pollution levels. He supported spending tens of millions of dollars on wildlife habitat restoration, state parks, and recreational trails; he signed a U.S.–Canadian pact to protect Lake Superior from industrial waste, and encouraged a more efficient, community-oriented Minnesota Pollution Control Agency (MPCA).

Carlson's brand of environmentalism was pragmatic rather than ideologically pure. "To assume that growth or business or economic development is hostile to the environment is preposterous," he said. "You're never going to get back the earth the way it was prior to the advent of man. But you can certainly make very rational choices. What we have focused on is outcomes, and by that I mean what we have to do to protect or enhance the quality of our physical environment."

After growing up in the Bronx, Carlson saw his first lake when he came to Minnesota to attend graduate school, said Cindy Jepsen, a former deputy chief of staff who spearheaded his first-term environmental agenda. On an outing to a Minneapolis lake with friends, he couldn't believe that they wanted to leave because the beach was too crowded. How could there possibly be another like it in the entire city? "He was awestruck by the simple beauty of it," Jepsen said, "even though it was in the middle of an urban area, and that began, I think, the making of the environmental man."

Guests at annual Wild Game Dinners held at the Governor's Residence have been transfixed as Carlson spoke with the zealousness of a convert about outdoor pleasures—hunting, fishing, canoeing, bird watching, lakeside lounging—that many Minnesotans take for granted. "His main thrust in the environment is protecting the resources of Minnesota for the people to enjoy," said Ed Stringer, Carlson's chief of staff from 1992 to 1994, "for ordinary folks to get out in their campers and go to a park and put up their tents and cook an outdoor meal."

As he had on other issues, Carlson moved his environmental agenda forward by developing a coalition of like-minded individuals and organizations. On the environment, he reached out to sports enthusiasts, environmental advocates, farmers, business leaders, and ordinary citizens.

1991—WET AND WILD

Environmental activists didn't know what to think of Arne Carlson at first. He had sponsored key energy conservation and hazardous waste bills as a legislator in the 1970s, but he earned a reputation for tight-fistedness as state auditor. Some balked at his choice of Chuck Williams to head the Minnesota Pollution Control Agency. In the 1970s, Williams was a midlevel manager at Reserve Mining, a now-defunct company that was embroiled in a long-running, bitter dispute with the MPCA over the dumping of taconite tailings into Lake Superior. When he became MPCA commissioner, the self-described "hard-rock mining guy" decorated his office with photos of giant ore shovels.

"Chuck didn't exactly come in with a halo," Jepsen said.

Plain-spoken and workman-like in his short-sleeved, open-neck shirts, Williams immediately displayed his hands-on style by making frequent visits to industrial sites such as Ashland Refinery in St. Paul Park, quizzing plant managers about the latest emissions control technology, and telling war stories about mining on the Range.

It didn't take him long to stir controversy by questioning the introduction of state auto-emissions testing, but he quickly allayed concerns that he was out to gut the MPCA. The agency simply needed to be more efficient, and more responsive to the businesses forced to negotiate its regulatory maze in order to comply with pollution laws. "My charge from the governor was to change the focus of the agency from command-and-control to one of helping people to understand what the law is, and giving them whatever technical help they needed to get up to speed," Williams said.

By that summer, after a fierce legislative battle over a dwindling natural resource, Carlson achieved his first environmental victory, one of few legislative wins in 1991. Passage of the 1991 Wetlands Conservation Act, which established a "no-net-loss" policy on more than 3.5 million acres of marshes, fens, bogs, and wet meadows, made Minnesota a national leader in extending such strong protection to wetlands and the rich tapestry of living things that they support.

Carlson had come to appreciate wetlands as wildlife havens and buffers for flood control before he became governor. In the late 1980s, as secretary of Minnesota's Land Exchange Board, he championed the creation of Hamden Slough Wildlife Refuge in northwest Minnesota. Carlson knew that the state's roughly 8.7 million acres of wetlands—less than 60 percent of what had existed in frontier times—were disappearing fast under the plow and bulldozer. "When the governor came into office, the very first thing I remember him identifying in his environmental agenda was that we were going to pass the Wetlands Conservation Act," said Ron Nargang, deputy commissioner of the state Department of Natural Resources (DNR). "He was determined to see that done."

Wetlands bills had been proposed in both the 1989 and 1990 legislatures, but were killed by legislators, predominantly from rural areas, who saw wetlands protection as a threat to development, agriculture, and local sovereignty. This time around Representative Willard Munger, the Duluth DFLer renowned for his environmental advocacy, had a formidable ally in the governor's office. "Some of my fellow DFLers are ribbing me for supporting Governor Carlson's position, but this is the first time that any governor has stood up and fought for wetlands and put his money where his mouth is," Munger said at the time.

Jepsen, Nargang, and Ron Harnak, executive director of the state Board of Water and Soil Resources (BWSR), were Carlson's emissaries at the Capitol. Nargang and Harnak educated lawmakers on wetlands ecology, floodwater retention, and other technical issues. Jepsen handled the politics, cajoling lawmakers and trading favors to ensure that the bill cleared each hurdle on its way to the House and Senate floors. "It was the art of negotiation and of compromise," Jepsen said.

At one point, the wetlands bill was in danger of being scuttled in the Senate Environment and Natural Resources Committee, chaired by Senator Bob Lessard, DFL-International Falls. Piqued by Carlson's failure to mention him in his State of the State message, Lessard refused to schedule a hearing for the measure, or even talk to the governor or any of his staff. So Jepsen sent Lessard a note indicating that she had ordered beer for both of them. "So, if one beer softens you up a little, I'd still like to meet with you. And I'm even willing to buy the second time around," she wrote. A mollified Lessard wrote back, asking Jepsen to make an appointment with his secretary—and "bring along the rest of the six-pack."

A major sticking point was compensation for landowners who

agreed not to drain their marshes, sloughs, swamps, and bogs. Carlson asked legislators to provide more than $30 million to restore lost wetlands and pay farmers for acreage returned to nature. In the end, the legislature appropriated $17.1 million, including $12 million in new bonding. On June 4, 1991, Carlson signed the bill at the Minnesota National Wildlife Refuge Center in Bloomington, overlooking hundreds of acres of preserved and restored wetlands.

That year, Carlson also played a pivotal role in ratification of the Binational Program to Restore and Protect the Lake Superior Basin, a joint U.S.–Canadian pact that set a goal of eliminating discharges of mercury, PCBs, insecticides, and other toxic chemicals into the world's largest lake. Carlson lobbied hard for the agreement at a September Council of Great Lakes Governors' meeting in Milwaukee. John Engler of Michigan and Tommy Thompson of Wisconsin were concerned about the agreement's impact on paper milling, mining, and other lakeside industries.

At the end of the day, as the meeting was about to adjourn, a stroke of public relations genius won them over. Carlson's staff drew an outline map of the Great Lakes states, leaving space within the borders of each state for its governor's signature. Following Carlson's lead, Thompson and Engler signed, knowing that the document had no legal standing. Unveiled to the press later that week at a meeting of the International Joint Commission on the Great Lakes in Traverse City, Michigan, the map sealed the governors' commitment to a clean Lake Superior. Approval of the Binational Program formed the framework for an ongoing effort to rid all five Great Lakes of industrial pollutants.

Don Arnosti, Minnesota director of the National Audubon Society, believed the pact would have been doomed without Carlson's leadership. "He stood up for the Binational Agreement when all the other Republican governors were bolting ship," Arnosti said. In 1992, the society gave Carlson its Special Recognition Award for his efforts on behalf of Lake Superior and wetlands conservation.

RECLAIMING A FORGOTTEN RIVER

On September 22, 1992, standing on a bluff at the National Wildlife Refuge, the governor held up a jar of Minnesota River water to the light. The water was chocolate-colored, rendered virtually opaque by its heavy burden of sediment laced with fertilizers, pesticides, and raw sewage. Minnesota's namesake river was in sad shape. The 330-mile-long waterway that had once run clear over white sand and teemed with fish and waterfowl, had deteriorated into little more than an open sewer for the cities and farm operations along its banks. Carlson had come to the Wildlife Refuge to launch an ambitious, long-term, cleanup campaign for the Minnesota.

"Our goal is that within 10 years our children will be swimming, fishing, picnicking, and recreating at this river," he said. That pledge set in motion a multiagency, grassroots cleanup effort of unprecedented scope and vision. Over the next six years close to $1 billion in federal, state, local, and foundation funds were poured into the reclamation effort. Four state agencies and the U.S. Department of Agriculture worked with local governments, farmers, and city residents along the river to curb soil erosion, restore natural vegetation, and plug leaking manure lagoons and septic tanks.

At Carlson's urging, the 1993 legislature appropriated $500,000 annually for a Board of Water and Soil Resources (BWSR) cost-share program to promote soil conservation practices and feedlot cleanup. After floods devastated the Minnesota River Valley that spring, the board invested $7.6 million in Reinvest in Minnesota (RIM) Reserve and other state funds to enroll 9,200 low-lying acres of farmland in permanent conservation easements.

Meanwhile, over at the MPCA, Williams was transforming the agency —and incurring the ire of environmental activists. Groups such as Citizens for a Better Environment and Earth Protector, Inc., complained that Williams hadn't required comprehensive environmental studies for certain projects, including expansion of a potato-processing plant near Park Rapids and a $4.5 million golf course and housing development at Giant's

Ridge on the Iron Range. Unfazed, the commissioner pressed ahead with his mission to boost efficiency and make the agency more accountable to its customers—Minnesota companies obliged to comply with increasingly stringent and complex federal pollution laws. "The things that got accomplished there, the staff accomplished," Williams said. "My role was more as a catalyst for change."

"Fast-track" emissions permits eliminated much of the red tape that infuriated corporate environmental managers in the 1980s. To ensure prompt follow-through, Williams organized project reviewers into teams and directed them to resolve crucial environmental issues at the outset. Aware that developers were afraid to buy contaminated "brownfields" because of potential liability under federal Superfund laws, the MPCA afforded them protection from lawsuits under its Voluntary Investigation and Cleanup program. Between 1992 and 1998, more than 800 companies enrolled in the cleanup program, which won an award for governmental innovation from the Ford Foundation in 1994.

Williams, who resigned in 1996 to take a job with EVTAC Mining near Eveleth, Minnesota, also modernized information management at the agency. "When I got there people were using typewriters," he said. He also changed the MPCA's decidedly metro-centric mindset by transferring more than 50 employees from headquarters in St. Paul to five out-state offices.

HOW TO MAKE FRIENDS AND INFLUENCE LEGISLATORS

Despite a chronic financial crisis during his first term, Carlson managed to squeeze enough funds from the legislature to support critical, ongoing environmental initiatives, such as farmland-to-wildlife programs and expansion of state parks and recreational trails. Often the governor's staff and department heads relied on environmental and sporting organizations for lobbying assistance. From the beginning, Carlson reached out to hunters, anglers, farmers, conservationists, canoeists, bird watchers—anybody who could exert pressure on budget-conscious lawmakers.

"I don't think there's any doubt that the governor has slowly and systematically built a great deal of confidence in those groups," Ron Nargang said. Letters and phone calls from hunters and anglers helped fulfill Carlson's campaign pledge to restore funding for RIM Reserve, a program that had transformed tens of thousands of acres of marginal crop land into wildlife habitat. In 1990, only $750,000 was appropriated for RIM; by 1994, the program boasted a budget of $4.5 million.

Alliances with the Minnesota Parks and Trails Council, the Nature Conservancy, the Audubon Society, and other outdoor groups helped secure $16.3 million in the 1993 and 1994 sessions for the development of two new state parks (Grand Portage and Glendalough), statewide land acquisitions and improvements, and extensions of several state trails, including the North Shore snowmobile trail and the Willard Munger bicycle trail.

With encouragement from the Department of Agriculture, the governor supported the nascent ethanol industry, a hotly debated issue in the early 1990s. In 1991 and 1993, when the legislature passed bills requiring ethanol blends at the gas pump and expanding producer payments, Carlson signed them. By the end of 1997, 11 ethanol production plants operated in the state, producing more than 150 million gallons of renewable ethanol and 460,000 tons of dried distillers grains from 57 million bushels of Minnesota corn.

"When push came to shove, he was there, and really helped it work," said Ralph Groschen, senior marketing specialist with the state Department of Agriculture. As a result, the Twin Cities met federal standards for carbon monoxide emissions every year between 1992 and 1998.

Carlson butted heads with many environmental groups in 1994 during one of the most divisive legislative sessions in decades. Northern States Power Company was seeking permission to store radioactive waste in 17 sealed casks at its Prairie Island nuclear plant near Red Wing. NSP argued that above-ground storage was necessary to avoid an early shutdown of the plant that would cost hundreds of jobs and millions of dollars in higher utility bills. A phalanx of environmental groups and the nearby Prairie Island Dakota Community adamantly opposed the idea, evoking fears of unnatural catastrophe on the banks of the

CAMP PHOTOS COURTESY OF TED AYERS

PHOTO COURTESY OF WILLIAMS COLLEGE ARCHIVES AND SPECIAL COLLECTIONS

Clockwise from the top left: Governor Carlson with his mother Kerstin. Kerstin Carlson's emphasis on creating educational opportunities for her sons was one of the driving forces in the development of Governor Carlson's zeal for education reform.

Campers at St. Andrew's Camp in Wallingford, Conn., lined up for tent inspection in the summer of 1944. Arne Carlson, far left, was a rookie camper that year. His brother Sten Carlson, second from right, also attended.

The campers shared a swimming hole with a neighboring farmer's cows. Arne Carlson, far right in the third row, joined the swimmers in 1946.

In 1957, Carlson graduated from Williams College, and he soon went to work for U.S. Senator Hubert H. Humphrey.

Clockwise from the top: Carlson's core campaign group for the "second campaign" in 1990 included, (front from left to right), Craig Shaver, Joanell Dyrstad, Marvin Dyrstad; (back from left to right), Len Hardwick, Ruth Grendahl, Scott Day, Bob Anderson, Arne Carlson, Lars Carlson, and Lois Mack.

A rally at Macalester College and a candlelight vigil at the Governor's Residence were among the flurry of campaign events for Carlson and running mate Joanell Dyrstad.

Election night was a long night for Carlson and his supporters. The next morning, Susan and Arne Carlson, and Joanell and Marvin Dyrstad, met with supporters like Wheelock Whitney (center) to celebrate victory.

Discussing the campaign's media strategy during a packed reception on Halloween night, 1990, are (left to right), Len Hardwick, Paul Anderson, and Lars Carlson.

From the top: In July 1991, Carlson welcomed Arnold Schwartzenegger to Minnesota for the Special Olympics. Carlson's backing has been instrumental in bringing films and theater to Minnesota.

Workers' compensation was an area that desperately needed reform when Governor Carlson took office. Here, on January 30, 1992, the Governor talks to residents about the issue on a whistle-stop tour through Detroit Lakes.

On Lake of the Woods in August 1993. Front, (left to right), Personal Assistant Mary Thomas, Press Secretary Cyndy Brucato, Arne Carlson, and Susan Carlson. Back, left to right, State Trooper Pete Tiegen, Director of Tourism Hank Todd, and *Star Tribune* reporter Bob Whereatt.

Clockwise from the top: Governor Carlson welcomes a bunny to his Halloween Open House. The Carlsons opened the Governor's Residence many times throughout the year for children and families to enjoy.

Governor Carlson meets the press for the first time.

Visiting with school children has always been a joy for Carlson, who met with students frequently throughout his years in office.

Governor Carlson met with Bob Dole during an April 1993 visit.

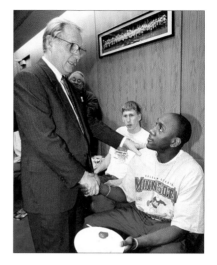

Clockwise from the top: One of the most elegant events held at the Governor's Residence during Carlson's years in office was the wedding reception of his daughter Anne to Andrew Davis in April 1993.

Carlson gives some advice to Gopher Bobby Jackson.

Carlson often focused on preserving outdoor recreational activities for all Minnesotans.

Carlson and Gopher Coach Clem Haskins have been friends since Haskins first came to Minnesota in 1985.

This column, from the top: The Carlsons often challenge Minnesota students to read more. During the 1994 campaign, First Lady Susan Carlson read to children at the St. James Public Library.

Victory! November 8, 1994. Governor Carlson was reelected by a landslide. Celebrating are from left to right, Jessica Carlson, Susan Carlson, Arne Carlson, former Lieutenant Governor Joanell Dyrstad, incoming Lieutenant Governor Joanne Benson, and her husband Bob Benson.

This column, from the top: Arne and Lars Carlson celebrated the opening of the Children's Garden at the Governor's Residence in July 1993.

Meeting a Swedish governor was a big thrill for Ann Margaret, who was in Minnesota for the filming of *Grumpier Old Men* in 1995. Co-star Jack Lemmon posed with Margaret and the Carlsons.

From the top: Governor Carlson joins former Minnesota governors during a holiday celebration in 1993. Front row from left to right, wife of former Governor Harold LeVander (1967-1971), Iantha LeVander, former Governor Al Quie (1979-1983), former Governor C. Elmer Anderson (1951-1955), and former Governor Harold Stassen (1939-1943). Back row from left to right, Arne Carlson, Ginny Stringer, wife of Ed Stringer, Chief of Staff Ed Stringer, Lieutenant Governor Joanell Dyrstad.

Governor Carlson, supporters, friends, and staff gathered at the Governor's Residence in July 1994 to wish Ed Stringer well as he moved from Chief of Staff to Supreme Court Justice. From left to right, Residence Director Barb Hoffmann, Ed Stringer, and Ginny Stringer, wife of Ed Stringer.

Clockwise from the top: In May 1994, the Carlsons welcome a student group to the Governor's Residence.

Supreme Court Chief Justice A.M. "Sandy" Keith and Appeals Court Chief Judge Anne Simonett administer the oath of office to Carlson in January 1995. Susan Carlson, daughter Jessica Carlson, and son-in-law, Andrew Davis look on.

Reporters clamored around Carlson for a comment on Election Night 1994. Carlson's victory over Democrat John Marty was the second biggest landslide in Minnesota history.

Susan Carlson has been a judicial referee since May 1995. Her time as a referee has been instrumental in the growth of her understanding of Fetal Alcohol Syndrome and has led her to champion the fight against it.

Susan Carlson with P.J. Huggabee bears. With support from Dayton's, the program donates one bear per bear sold to a child going into foster care. Originated by Illinois First Lady Brenda Edgar, the program came to Minnesota in September 1995.

This column, from the top: From left to right, Governor Ann Richards of Texas and Governor Tommy Thompson of Wisconsin listen to Governor Carlson at an annual winter meeting of the National Governor's Association in Washington, D.C., on January 31, 1994.

On September 16, 1996, Governor Carlson, always proud of his Swedish heritage, welcomes the King and Queen of Sweden to the Governor's Residence. From left to right, Arne Carlson, King Carl Gustaf, Kerstin Carlson (the Governor's mother), and Queen Silvia.

In December 1996, Governor Carlson meets with children at the annual Governor's Residence Christmas party. The Governor often invites children from a local elementary school to sing songs and meet with Santa.

This column from the top: The Gophers' Number One fans, Arne and Susan Carlson, cheer on the men's basketball team at the NCAA Final Four.

Morrie Anderson says goodbye at a farewell dinner given in his honor at the Governor's Residence on August 12, 1997. A trusted friend and Chief of Staff, Anderson moved on to become the Interim Chancellor at the Minnesota State Colleges and Universities.

PHOTO COURTESY OF STAR TRIBUNE

From the top: As his accomplishments increased, Carlson's confidence as governor grew. During his State of the State Address in 1997, he outlined a bold plan for education reform.

Children joined Carlson for the signing of the 1997 school choice bill in the Children's Garden at the residence.

Although Governor Carlson is well known for wielding his veto power, he has signed many more bills than he has vetoed. Here, he signs a bill at his desk in May 1997.

Left Column: On May 9, 1997, Susan and Arne Carlson welcome former British Prime Minister Margaret Thatcher to the Governor's Residence.

The First Family, September 13, 1997. Since moving into the Residence in 1991, both Anne Carlson Davis and Tucker Carlson were married there. From left to right, Arne Carlson, Jessica Carlson, Susan Carlson, Tucker Carlson, Monica (Duvall) Carlson, Anne Carlson Davis holding Drew Davis, Allie Davis, and Andrew Davis.

Mary Thomas, Governor Carlson's Personal Assistant and Governor Carlson. Along with her numerous official duties, Mary served as a trusted confidant and loyal friend.

Above: On October 8, 1997, Governor Carlson appointed Jim Gilbert to the Supreme Court and appointed Kathleen Blatz the first woman Chief Justice of the Minnesota Supreme Court. Governor Carlson is in the foreground. In back from left to right, Justices Alan Page, Esther Tomljanovich, Chief Justice Sandy Keith, Sandra Gardebring, Jim Gilbert, and Kathleen Blatz.

From the top: On May 8, 1998, high school band members in Hastings wish Governor Carlson good luck before he boards the boat that will take him to his last fishing opener in Red Wing, and his last chance to catch a fish at the opener. Their good wishes had an effect because he did catch a fish.

In 1998, Carlson visited China to encourage international trade for Minnesota companies. Carlson met with Chinese President Jiang Zemin. He was the second governor to have an audience with Jiang.

PHOTO COURTESY OF SCOTT AMUNDSON

Top: April 9, 1998. Negotiations wind down during the final, tense hours of the 1998 legislative session. From left to right, Press Secretary Jackie Renner, Chief of Staff Bernie Omann, Arne Carlson, Finance Commissioner Wayne Simoneau.

Above: On August 22, 1997, following a special legislative session to address the disastrous spring flooding earlier in the year, Governor Carlson signed an unprecedented $124 million flood relief package to help restore financial stability to flood-stricken areas. From left to right, Arne Carlson, Deputy Chief of Staff John Dyke, and Executive Secretary Susan Kalpak.

Above: In 1998, Governor Carlson's budget (which won legislative approval) allocated a record $206 million to the University of Minnesota for building renovations and construction. At the June dedication ceremony, are (left to right), House Speaker Phil Carruthers, Arne Carlson, and University of Minnesota President Mark Yudof.

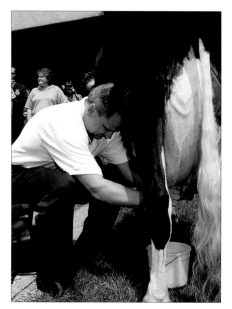

Clockwise from top left: Chief of Staff Bernie Omann in a cow-milking contest at the Minnesota Department of Agriculture in June 1998.

On March 4, 1998, Governor Carlson opens the Computers for Schools program with the Detwiler Foundation at the Stillwater Correctional Facility. Left to right, Commissioner of Corrections Fred LaFleur, Arne Carlson, and Assistant Commissioner Janet Entzel.

Governor Carlson meets weekly with staff members. On a Monday morning in April, 1998, they are (clockwise) Arne Carlson, Lieutenant Governor Joanne Benson, Legal Counsel Tanja Kozicky, Finance Commissioner Wayne Simoneau, Chief of Staff Bernie Omann, Deputy Press Secretary Valerie Gunderson, Director of Federal Relations Todd Johnson, Director of Strategic Planning Tim Sullivan, Deputy Chief of Staff John Dyke, and Executive Secretary Susan Kalpak.

PHOTO COURTESY OF SCOTT AMUNDSON

PHOTO COURTESY OF SCOTT AMUNDSON

On April 9, 1998, Governor Carlson and St. Paul Mayor Norm Coleman await word on negotiations on the 1998 bonding bill which included a new RiverCentre arena for St. Paul.

Arne Carlson says goodbye to legislators on the floor of the Senate on the final night of the 1998 legislative session.

Throughout his two terms, Governor Carlson has honored many leading Minnesota businesses and business people at the Governor's Residence. At a gathering on July 30, 1998, Governor Carlson and Susan hosted a reception for Wheelock Whitney. From left to right, Wheelock Whitney, Susan Carlson, Arne Carlson, Ellis Naegele, and Bob Naegele.

From the top: Governor Carlson, Minnesota Wild CEO Jac Sperling, Minnesota Wild Chairman Bob Naegele, and St. Paul Mayor Norm Coleman take a shot at the groundbreaking for the new St. Paul RiverCentre which will include a new hockey arena for the Minnesota Wild.

Above: Corporal Timothy Bowe, a 15-year veteran of the Minnesota State Patrol and former official state driver for Governor Carlson, was killed in the line of duty on Saturday, June 7, 1997. He worked on the Governor's Security Detail from 1993-1994 and again in 1996 where he was a driver for the Governor as well as Susan and Jessica Carlson. Governor Carlson considered him one of the finest law enforcement officers in Minnesota as well as a friend.

House Minority Leader Steve Sviggum following on the heels of Terry Dempsey, convinced the IR caucus to ultimately uphold all of Governor Carlson's 179 vetoes, including the critical Education bill veto in 1997. In back from left to right, CFL Commissioner Bob Wedl, Finance Commissioner Wayne Simoneau, and Arne Carlson.

Mississippi.

The governor supported NSP's request, and ultimately signed a bill authorizing dry-cask storage at the plant. It was a pragmatic decision. For him, the decision came down to economics—Minnesotans pay less than the national average for electricity, thanks in part to nuclear power—and the hard realities imposed by the lack of a permanent repository for nuclear waste.

"The federal government reneged on its promise to take care of disposing of nuclear waste," Carlson said, looking back at the debate. "What was NSP supposed to do? Close the plant down? How would we have replaced that cheap power?"

SUSTAINING MOMENTUM IN THE SECOND TERM

In March 1994, Minnesotans of every political persuasion gathered at the Minneapolis Convention Center for a conference called the Congress on Sustainable Development. Seven citizens' committees appointed by the governor and the state Environmental Quality Board reported on the status of farming, forestry, recreation, urban settlement, manufacturing, and other aspects of life in Minnesota. They concluded that you don't have to sacrifice greenery and wildlife on the altar of economic progress. It's possible to have a high standard of living, thriving communities, and a healthful, ecologically balanced environment.

This notion of sustainable development guided the governor's environmental agenda in his second term. Governmentally imposed, by-the-numbers regulation was out. A holistic, practical approach that let local communities and businesses share responsibility for environmental protection was in. Through its Minnesota Sustainable Development Initiative, the administration found common ground with people who liked to solve their own environmental problems—a diverse constituency of farmers, out-state civic leaders, business owners, and ordinary citizens that wasn't afraid to make itself heard in the legislature.

The cleansing of the Minnesota River was the best example of this grassroots strategy. The state found a way to attack pollution without depriving farmers of a living, or causing hardship for riverside businesses and residents. Early in 1994, the results of a four-year, $3 million study by more than 30 federal, state, and local agencies revealed the full extent of the Minnesota's degradation. Phosphorus, nitrogen, and other nutrients washed into the river from farm fields, harming aquatic plants and fish. Bacteria-laden sewage from feedlots and leaking septic tanks made swimming unhealthy. Carlson and his department heads knew that nothing could be done about such "non-point-source" pollution without the cooperation of local officials, businesses, and thousands of individual landowners.

To gain their support, open houses were held during the spring in Eden Prairie, Mankato, Redwood Falls, and Montevideo. These meetings, hosted by a 30-member citizens' advisory committee, proved a catalyst for enduring change in the Minnesota River Valley. City residents learned how overfertilizing lawns and dumping antifreeze in the street contributed to pollution. Farmers were assured that they wouldn't be slapped with heavy penalties as long as they acted in good faith to safeguard the river.

"Most people want to be good to what they regard as their physical environment," said Carlson. "If somebody can help farmers understand the technology of proper disposal of animal waste, for example, more often than not they're very willing to participate. We tend to forget that farmers are also people who fish and hunt and like wildlife."

Those attending the meetings grew into a constituency for the long-neglected Minnesota River—friends at city hall, in corporate offices, and on the land who could urge the legislature to get serious about cleaning up the river. There was already reason for hope; tests of river water in Mankato showed that it carried 25 percent less sediment than it had a decade earlier, mainly because of conservation tillage practices promoted by the agriculture department and the University of Minnesota. The formation of the Minnesota River Basin Joint Powers Board in 1995 focused the reclamation effort, coordinating projects by dozens of local governmental units and citizens groups in 37 counties. "What the Carlson administration can take credit for is having the foresight to pull in a basin-wide organization to do the restoration plan from the bottom up, rather than have a state-down approach," said Stephen Hansen, executive director of the board.

The state also provided financial support for local initiatives. The 1996 bonding bill included $5.8 million in RIM Reserve funds for wildlife habitat restoration along the banks of the Minnesota and its tributaries. Row crops such as corn and soybeans were replaced with trees, native grasses, and wetland plants that formed natural, sediment-trapping buffer strips. In the same year, the MPCA's Clean Water Partnership program dispensed $1.5 million in grants and loans for cleanup projects in the Minnesota River Basin. Other, ongoing environmental programs in the valley included the Board of Water and Soil Resources' cost-share program, which provided up to a 75 percent match for projects undertaken by private landowners; a state revolving fund for the repair of residential septic tanks; and the River-Friendly Farmer Program, a multiagency project that recognized farmers who had taken steps to minimize polluted runoff from their land.

Carlson's drive to clean up the Minnesota River earned him the National Great Blue Heron Award in 1995 from the North American Waterfowl Management Plan because of the river cleanup's positive effect on the health of waterfowl and other migratory bird populations.

NOT THE SAME OLD REGULATIONS

The concept of sustainable development also inspired major initiatives at the MPCA and the DNR. "We were trying to figure out how we could meet our environmental goals without interfering with communities meeting their goals, or businesses meeting theirs," said Peder Larson, who succeeded Williams as MPCA commissioner.

Regulatory Innovation, launched in the fall of 1996, offered an alternative to the long-winded, confusing, permitting process Minnesota manufacturers had been subjected to for the past 25 years. Instead of demanding separate emission permits for air, water, and solid and hazardous wastes, the agency began issuing customized, single permits that gave companies more leeway in compliance while still holding them to a high standard.

Rahr Malting Company, a producer of malted barley for the beer industry, began to operate under an MPCA emission permit that allowed it to boost its output without degrading the environment. In fact, the stretch of Minnesota River that flows past Rahr's Shakopee facility was cleaner a year after the permit was granted in 1997 than it had been before.

Anticipating higher discharges of phosphorus and other pollutants into the river from an on-site wastewater treatment plant that the company wanted to build, Rahr offset those future releases by "trading" emissions with the city of New Ulm. Farming on city land was eroding the riverbanks, dumping more than 3,000 tons of sediment annually into the river. Rahr paid the city to place a permanent conservation easement on the land and plant trees and prairie grass, dramatically reducing runoff. "The winner in that trade was the river," said Robert Micheletti, Rahr's vice president of operations.

At the DNR, passage of the Sustainable Forest Resources Act was Commissioner Rod Sando's top legislative priority in 1995. Sando served the entire eight years of Carlson's administration lending great continuity to the work of DNR. The culmination of a five-year environmental- impact study of timber harvesting in state forests, the act gave Minnesotans spanning a broad spectrum of interests a say in how the agency manages woodlands. Foresters, commercial loggers, resort owners, private landowners, and representatives of the Nature Conservancy and Audubon Society sat on the 14-member Minnesota Forest Resources Council, a policy advisory group. The council took a strong interest in regeneration of white pine, a valuable species that once covered vast swaths of northern Minnesota. The legislature approved a total of $2.1 million for white-pine regeneration in the 1997 and 1998 sessions.

A similar meeting of the minds was crucial to the survival of the Wetlands Conservation Act, which came under concerted attack in the 1995 and 1996 legislative sessions. Amendments

that would have severely weakened the act failed on a technical-
ity in 1995, but the following year a groundswell of opposition to
continued wetlands protection rolled into St. Paul. Elected officials from soggy northern Minnesota, many of whom had refused
to enforce the law, argued that the act allowed state regulators to
usurp their authority.

"Beltrami and the other northern counties have been good
stewards of the land," Beltrami County Commissioner Richard
Florhaug told the *Star Tribune*. "We've still got more than 80 percent of our wetlands. It's the Twin Cities area and the southern
part of Minnesota that have destroyed their wetlands. Yet, [state
regulators] want to treat all wetlands alike, and you can't. In the
metro area they talk about wetlands in square feet; up here we
talk about them in square miles." Farmers and developers complained that the law's "no-net-loss" provision, which required
destroyed wetlands to be replaced by an equal or greater acreage
of wetlands elsewhere, unfairly impinged on their livelihoods.

Carlson vowed to veto any bill that would significantly under-
mine wetlands conservation. Clearly concessions would have to
be made to rural interests in the upcoming session. The governor
laid the foundation for compromise by inviting more than 50
local officials, legislators, conservationists, and representatives of
agribusiness, logging, mining, and construction to a "stakehold-
ers' roundtable" in St. Cloud. Exhorted by Carlson to "work hard
at a resolution of the key issues," the participants did just that,
holing up in the St. Cloud Holiday Inn for three days in early
January. A rough consensus emerged that formed the framework
for a new, more flexible wetlands law that retained the spirit of
the original. "The governor's support of a wetlands roundtable
really made the difference," said Harnak of the Board of Water
and Soil Resources.

The revamped act gave local counties, municipalities, and soil
and water districts more authority over wetlands management,
eased protection of seasonally flooded basins and wet meadows,
and allowed very small wetlands to be filled or drained without
replacement. The package maintained the state's "no-net-loss"
policy, a key issue for Carlson. Taken to task once again by

Representative Willard Munger, and mindful of Carlson's veto threat, legislators agreed to maintain strong protection for most types of wetlands, and provide $3 million in bond revenue to restore drained wetlands and buy protective easements on existing wetlands.

OUT WITH A BANG

Toward the end of his administration, Carlson struck two more blows for Minnesota's environment. The governor's vision of a swimmable, fishable Minnesota River by early in the twenty-first century came into sharp focus on February 19, 1998, at the National Wildlife Refuge in Bloomington. Carlson and U.S. Department of Agriculture Deputy Secretary Richard Rominger signed a state-federal pact that would remove up to 190,000 acres of environmentally sensitive, flood-prone land in the Minnesota River Valley from agricultural production. Originally conceived as a state initiative, the campaign to restore the river now had the backing of the federal government.

Tim Searchinger, a senior attorney with the Environmental Defense Fund in Washington, D.C., said that the agreement made the cleanup of the Minnesota River "far and away the largest effort to restore the natural wetlands and floodplains of a river," a project comparable in size to the much better publicized campaign to rehabilitate Maryland's Chesapeake Bay.

It was Searchinger who contacted the Board of Water and Soil Resources in 1996, suggesting that the agency apply for federal Conservation Reserve Program funds to buy conservation easements along the Minnesota. The USDA has pledged $100 million to the Minnesota River Watershed Conservation Reserve Enhancement Program to enroll eligible farmland in 15-year Conservation Reserve Program contracts. State officials hoped that much of that acreage would roll over into perpetual or long-term easements funded through RIM Reserve.

Victory for the river came only after two years of intense lobbying by Carlson and Board of Water and Soil Resources officials. Proposed by Carlson in the fall of 1996, the Enhancement Program immediately ran into opposition from farm groups that objected to the notion of farmers relinquishing control of their land. Carlson countered persuasively in a letter to then–Agriculture Secretary Dan Glickman that his proposal would actually save USDA money by blunting the impact of floods like those that ravaged the Minnesota River Valley in 1993 and 1997. Hansen, of the Minnesota River Basin Joint Powers Board, said, "He was very instrumental in getting across the idea that this is a one-time investment that takes the land out of production so that we don't lose the soil, and don't have to pay restitution to farmers who have lost their crops."

Also in 1998, Carlson presented to lawmakers the Access to the Outdoors environmental bonding package. The package, the largest in state history, called for $201 million in spending for enhancing wildlife habitat, extending the network of recreational trails, sprucing up state and regional parks and expanding opportunities for hunting and fishing. More than a dozen environmental organizations, including the Minnesota Parks and Trails Council, the Nature Conservancy, the Audubon Society, Ducks Unlimited, and Pheasants Forever, worked with Carlson staffer Tim Sullivan to develop the package. The proposal grew out of Carlson's sense that the outdoors is a unique part of Minnesota's identity and needed to be preserved. "Part of being a Minnesotan is being outdoors," said Carlson, an avid boater. In addition, recreation was an important part of the state's economy. Fishing alone pumped $1 billion a year into the state's economy, Carlson noted when he announced the plan at Fort Snelling State Park in December 1997.

Many of the park buildings, roads, and utility systems had been built in the Depression and needed repair. Carlson also wanted to create a one-stop shopping system for citizens seeking recreational licenses, like fishing licenses or park permits.

"Finally he had a wonderful budget surplus and was able to do some things that he really believed in," said Dorian Grilley, executive director of the Parks and Trails Council. The legislature ultimately passed a $141 million appropriation that retained most of his recommendations.

There were disappointments as well. Carlson's proposal to

establish a World War II veterans memorial park on Duluth's waterfront sank when city residents objected to the proposed location and size of its centerpiece, a decommissioned U.S. Navy heavy cruiser. But $59 million was approved for new visitor centers at Itasca, Mille Lacs, Kathio, and Forestville state parks, systemwide improvements to campgrounds, boat landings, and other facilities, and about 70 miles of new bicycling, hiking, inline skating, and snowmobiling trails.

THE JOURNEY CONTINUES

How will history rate Carlson's environmental record?

"He'll probably get too much credit for his fiscal adeptness and not enough for his environmental initiatives," said Gene Merriam, the former Coon Rapids DFLer who chaired the Senate's Environment and Natural Resources Committee for six years.

Nevertheless, Carlson made an imprint on Minnesota's environment. In the Carlson era, hundreds of acres of wetlands were saved from drainage and development. The Minnesota River began to purge itself of a century-old load of filth. Expansion of state parks and trails allowed more Minnesotans to enjoy the outdoors. And state agencies such as the MPCA and DNR became much more attuned to the concerns of local communities and businesses. Overall, the environmental machinery runs more efficiently than it did a decade ago.

Carlson saw his administration as part of a continuum of environmental stewardship that began at the turn of the century when another Republican expanded the nation's forests and shielded national parks such as Yellowstone and Yosemite from development.

"When Theodore Roosevelt opened up the notion that government has a role to play in defining our physical well-being related to the outside, that was just the start of a journey that has no end," Carlson said. "All any governor can do is be a part of that journey."

CHAPTER ELEVEN

A '90S CAMPAIGN

Avoiding Attacks from the Left and Right, Carlson Wins Landslide

A reelection campaign was not always a given during Arne Carlson's first term as governor. After his victory in 1990, his popularity ratings sank. The lowest of the lows came in the summer of 1992. Only 22 percent of Minnesotans viewed the governor in a positive light. For 18 months, he had been beaten up in the media and on the floor of the legislature as he struggled to bring the state's fiscal house to order. It got so bad Susan Carlson joked to friends that she came from the home of a battered governor.

So in September 1992, Carlson and a group of advisers met in the basement of the Governor's Residence to consider the future. It was a mixed group. It included top staff such as policy adviser Ed Stringer and Chief of Staff John Riley, who, suffering from brain cancer, was in his last weeks with the governor. Legislators Kathleen Blatz and Roy Terwilliger attended, as well as political stalwarts from the first campaign, like former legislator Craig Shaver and the governor's brother Lars Carlson. Research done for the group by marketing consultant Len Hardwick showed that voters knew little about Carlson's philosophy or politics. They did not know what he stood for, besides cutting budgets. Carlson had passed a health care plan in the 1992 session and progress had been made on workers' compensation reform. The governor knew that unless he turned things around politically the rest of his original agenda could be in danger. By the end of the 1993 legislative session, gubernatorial candidates for 1994 would be positioning themselves. Without an improvement in his political standing, a reelection run might be impossible.

The group talked at length about what Carlson needed to do to pull himself up in the polls and prepare for a reelection campaign. At issue was whether Carlson should take a "no-new-taxes" pledge. Such a pledge would require more budget cutting and might endanger social programs the governor wanted to pursue. Several advisers felt a no-new-taxes pledge was essential to define Carlson as a fiscally responsible governor.

As he often did, Carlson listened as his advisers argued the issue, sometimes vigorously.

"It was a break-left, break-right decision," recalled Craig Shaver. "The political people especially wanted him to break right because it would mean the difference between an easy ride in 1994 or disaster." Some of his policy advisers felt a tax increase might be the only way to fund the initiatives Carlson wanted to pursue.

"He surrounds himself at important times with a lot of smart, aggressive, outspoken people and watches the free-for-all," Shaver said. "He listens to it and then makes his decision. People with strong opinions are welcome here. If people enter the free-for-all intelligently and present well-reasoned arguments, they are welcome. Shrinking violets need not apply."

Carlson broke right and made "no new taxes" his hallmark from 1993 on. In addition, Carlson and the group agreed on three broad issues that would guide the administration's legislative program: jobs, kids, and quality of life. Said Ed Stringer, who became Carlson's chief of staff soon afterward, "We looked at all of the administration's proposals in that light—do they enhance jobs, do they make things better for kids, or do they improve quality of life. If not, we didn't do them. Rarely have I seen anything gel with such excitement and focus."

Within a few months, Carlson froze state employee salaries as the last sacrifice to get the state's financial house in order. His poll numbers spiked and by the spring of 1993, his approval ratings hit 59 percent, his highest rating since being elected. "That [1993] session was when a more serious effort began to define this governor," recalled then–Press Secretary Cyndy Brucato. "It showed that he stood first and foremost for fiscal responsibility, that he approached social policies with a pragmatic viewpoint, and that he was concerned about children and education. It was not a softhearted approach, but level-headed. It's simply what he was."

With encouragement from his wife, Susan, who had always wanted him to seek a second term, Carlson decided he definitely would run again. He had too much left to do.

TROUBLES WITH THE PARTY

Unlike his election in 1990, Carlson vowed to seek the endorsement of the Independent-Republican Party in 1994. As a sitting governor, who had been faced with a budget shortfall and significantly reduced state spending, Carlson felt he had earned the support of conservatives, even if they did not agree with him on every social issue. In the fall of 1993, he attended the party's off-year meeting in St. Cloud. Among the items on the agenda was a straw poll on gubernatorial preferences. Seven weeks earlier, a farmer and former legislator from St. Peter, Allen Quist, had entered the race. Quist had been one of the most socially conservative legislators in the House, noted largely for his long speeches against abortion and homosexuality. Quist promised the Republicans that he would represent "pro-life, pro-family, right-to-bear-arms people, tax protesters, and anti-establishment people."

Carlson wanted a win in St. Cloud. His relationship with the party had not improved much since 1990. A rejection in St. Cloud would devastate his 1994 campaign. So Carlson asked friends and cabinet members to attend the meeting, to bolster his cheering section, and to persuade delegates to support the governor. He threw a party for delegates—complete with a dance band and flashing lights—on the Friday night before the Saturday meeting at the St. Cloud Convention Center. When Carlson came into the meeting, supporters whooped and hollered and waved signs.

Carlson bolstered his conservative credentials by entering the meeting with Bernie Omann, a pro-life, popular, former central Minnesota legislator who was running for Congress in the 7th District. He also enlisted the support of prominent Republicans to encourage delegates not to dump the governor. U.S. Representative Jim Ramstad spoke for the governor, as did Senator David Durenberger and former Senator Rudy Boschwitz.

Carlson pleaded with the delegates to support him. "I make no bones about it. I need you," the governor said.

Then Carlson played his trump card: former U.S. Congressman Vin Weber, whom conservatives considered one of their brightest stars.

"The Democrats are in trouble," Weber told the crowd. "What's their hope? They want to read in the papers tomorrow that there was blood on the floor in St. Cloud."

Carlson earned 40 percent of the delegates' support to Quist's 37 percent. It was a narrow victory and a wake-up call.

"We knew then we could not bank on endorsement," Carlson said, "and Bernie recommended we bring on some people to look at our so-called political operation." They brought in four Minnesotans with broad political experience—Terri Ashmore, Dan Rice, Tim Sullivan, and Annette Meeks—to assess the campaign's voter identification programs and organizational efforts.

The four, along with veteran Washington consultant, Jim Nathanson, interviewed members of the governor's Kitchen Cabinet and campaign staff. They discovered an organization that was "technically naive," and hampered by an inability to make decisions and stick with them. Too often volunteer advisers distracted and redirected the campaign's effort, they found.

The group delivered its report to Carlson in person at his

Capitol office. No one else attended the session, and they had what Dan Rice described as "a blunt conversation."

"The analysis said, 'You're dead meat,'" Carlson recalled.

The campaign did not have an effective organization or a good database of likely supporters and voters. It needed to leap into the 1990s. Carlson made two crucial decisions late that fall. First, he determined that he would have to go to the primary election again to be the Republican candidate for governor. Second, he needed the best campaign director he could find to get him there. After a national search, Carlson hired a Minnesotan, Joe Weber.

Weber was the youngest brother of Vin Weber, and a political operative of renown. Weber had been a professional political organizer for nearly a decade. He served as regional political director for the National Republican Congressional Committee in California and had handled voter identification and contact for California Governor Pete Wilson. He could provide the decisive leadership the campaign needed.

"There was a recognition that the campaign needed to be reorganized," Weber said. "A lot of times with campaigns that's half the battle. You'll have a candidate that doesn't want to admit there's a problem. Arne reviewed the information he had and decided he needed to make changes."

The difference was immediate. "Joe comes on board and all of the sudden we have focus, we have technology, we have a game plan," Carlson recalled. "Things started to cook."

Carlson made one other change before the precinct caucuses in 1994. Lieutenant Governor Joanell Dyrstad announced that she would run for U.S. Senate to replace Durenberger. Carlson did not want Dyrstad to leave the ticket, but she was tired of the powerlessness that comes with the lieutenant governor's job. Two weeks after Dyrstad's announcement, Carlson and two busloads of supporters rolled into St. Cloud for a rally. Carlson introduced his new running mate, state Senator Joanne Benson. A pro-life legislator and former educator, Benson brought Carlson conservative credentials to help him with party activists. She also proved to be an exceptional stump politician, who loved to meet the crowds and shake hands.

A GENETIC PREDISPOSITION

Despite Carlson's improved organization and more conservative running mate, Quistian conservatives—as Quist supporters were called—dominated the March Republican caucuses. Many of the delegates elected to the county conventions and later to the state party convention were first-time caucus attendees who came out of evangelical Christian churches. Several long-time Republican activists and elected officials were shoved out of delegate spots to make way for the newcomers who supported Quist. Cal Ludeman, a staunch conservative who had been the party's nominee for governor in 1986, was denied a seat at the state convention, as was former House Minority Leader Bill Schrieber. Even Joanell Dyrstad was rejected as a delegate.

Several issues motivated the Quistians, including opposition to abortion, opposition to a gay rights bill Carlson had signed, and opposition to outcome-based education. In Allen Quist, they saw an articulate true believer that would take their message to the voters. A one-time college professor, Quist had a tendency to lecture and overexplain, which gave the Carlson camp an easy opportunity to define Quist in early April.

In an interview with the political reporter for the alternative weekly *Twin Cities Reader*, Quist discussed his views on marriage and gender equity. Men, he explained, had a "genetic predisposition" to head households. "You have a political arrangement in marriage," Quist said, "similar to any other political arrangement. And when push comes to shove, the higher level of political authority normally—I think there are exceptions—should be in the hands of the husband." When pressed as to why the authority should be with the husband, Quist responded, "I think there's a genetic predisposition."

Within days, several prominent Republican women—including former U.S. Ambassador Evie Teegen; state legislators Connie Morrison, Peggy Lippick, and Sidney Pauly; and former party chairwomen Carolyn Ring and Loanne Thrane—criticized Quist for the remark. Quist thinks women are inferior to men, they charged.

"We are offended that a serious political candidate of a major political party holds beliefs which demean 50 percent of the population," Teegen told a packed press conference.

Quist first claimed he was quoted out of context. Then he accused Carlson of "hiding behind these women." Finally, he called a press conference at which his wife, party activist Julie Quist, defended him. Still the expression "genetically predisposed" stuck and the idea that Quist disdained women haunted Quist through the rest of the campaign. And Quist never apologized or recanted the comment.

"He was so darn stubborn," said Cyndy Brucato. "All he needed to do was say, 'I made a mistake,' and it would go away. But he just kept defending himself."

While the genetic-predisposition controversy helped Carlson with the public, it did nothing to endear him to the delegates that would attend the Republican Party convention in June. Unlike 1990, Carlson could not ignore the party. He wanted to seek endorsement, although he knew he'd never get it.

"Our strategy was to participate in the process and be respectful of the process with the full and complete understanding that we were not going to get the endorsement," Weber said.

So Carlson went to the convention in June and delivered a speech that answered all of the misinformation that Quist supporters had circulated to discredit him. He also defended signing the gay rights bill, because "to do anything else would be discrimination." Veteran political reporter Bill Salisbury described the speech as "in your face."

The atmosphere was frosty. Cyndy Brucato remembered delegates looking at the Carlson entourage "suspiciously, as if we were doing something heinous and illegal." Even with backing from conservatives like Vin Weber and Omann, Quist trounced Carlson for the nomination.

Carlson "carried it off with a great deal of dignity," Brucato said. "He was very resigned to it. He had faith in his staff and the campaign and faith in himself. He thought he deserved to be governor again."

"We really didn't mind being booed by the delegates," Weber said. That behavior led many reporters to portray Carlson as "a good Republican victimized by a party gone astray," Weber said. That message might not appeal to the party faithful, but to the 200,000 middle-of-the-road Republicans the governor wanted to turn out in the primary, it worked perfectly.

"A COMFORTABLE RIDE"

Carlson had two things in 1994 that he had desperately needed in 1990: money and organization. With Republican activists Wheelock Whitney and Maureen Shaver running the finance operation, the governor had plenty of cash. He raised close to $2 million before the campaign ended in November. He also had all the technology and organization needed to ensure that his supporters made it to the polls. It was a '90s campaign.

The campaign's research showed that Carlson's chances of winning the primary improved as turnout increased. So, the campaign worked with businesses to encourage get-out-the-vote efforts. Led by Pierson "Sandy" Grieve, then the chairman and chief executive officer of Ecolab, Inc., the efforts did not mention voting for Carlson—just voting. Banks around town agreed to flash "don't forget to vote" messages on their automatic teller machines. Other companies encouraged employees to vote through employee newsletters.

Finally, Carlson was determined to define Quist in voters' mind. One advertisement called "Win" reminded voters that Quist "wants to regulate every aspect of our lives, even what we think." The ad recalled Quist's "genetic predisposition" statement by flashing headlines from newspapers and magazines. One read: "Fear of Quist's agenda persists." The ad concluded with the statement, "If he wins, we all lose." Carlson also moved the quick-tongued Brucato from his office staff to the campaign. "It took her 16 seconds to get her six-gun out and blaze away at Quist," the governor said.

The strategy worked, almost too well. Having a competitive primary guaranteed a candidate an additional $300,000 in state funding, if he agreed to abide by state campaign finance limits. As votes rolled in on primary election night, Joe Weber pulled Wheelock Whitney aside to express his concern about what to do if they beat Quist by more than two to one, the state definition of a competitive primary. "I had already spent that $300,000," Weber said. In the end, Carlson got 66 percent of the vote, but was 2,500 votes short of the two-to-one limit.

While Quist and Carlson dueled, the DFL had its own internal battles. A three-way primary left state Senator John Marty, one of the most liberal members of the Minnesota Legislature, as the DFL candidate. Having defeated Quist on the right and facing Marty on the left, Carlson easily held on to the middle ground.

"Our basic agenda was a general election campaign from the beginning," Weber said. "We knew from research that we did not need to move further to the center to appeal to a broader group of voters. We just needed to keep Marty way to the left."

Marty helped them do that by proposing an elaborate expansion of social programs and a tax cut at the same time. You could not do both and stay solvent. Brucato continued to tongue-lash the governor's opponents, once saying Marty seemed to be running for class president, not governor. When Marty unveiled his $150 million tax rebate, Brucato sniped, "My 6-year-old on his Ninja Turtle computer can figure out that this does not add up." At the seven debates Carlson and Marty held, the governor pounded away at Marty's inconsistencies. Each week, the Carlson campaign polls showed Carlson steadily increasing his lead over Marty.

Campaigns can be grueling and destructive to candidates, Carlson said. Not this one. The campaign scheduled events in such a way that Carlson had time to spend with his wife and children. It did not barrage him with details or internal conflicts. Through most of the 1994 campaign, Carlson worked strictly with three people: Weber, Brucato, and Whitney.

"I would come home at night and call Joe Weber," Carlson recalled. "He would give me the results of whatever polls we'd done that day. It was just very comfortable."

Marty proved to be a difficult candidate to manage. In the final two months of the campaign, he had three different campaign managers. The first of these, Bob Meeks, moaned to a reporter, "He'd rather be right than be governor."

By three o'clock on the afternoon of the election, Carlson knew he had won and by how much. "Everybody had very specific assignments," Carlson said of the 1994 campaign. "Everyone executed their assignment and I did not mess with it."

Carlson garnered more than 1.1 million votes, 64 percent of those cast, making his 1994 election the second biggest landslide in state history. (Only Hubert H. Humphrey had a bigger win when he defeated Jerry Brekke in a 1976 race for U.S. Senate.) The victory gave Carlson a new sense of confidence and a new tool to use in promoting his agenda. Now, he was a governor with a mandate.

CHAPTER TWELVE

CLOSING THE CIRCLE: EDUCATION

Carlson Helps Strengthen Programs "From Cradle to Career"

The governor looked tired and drained on the morning of May 21, 1997. The day before, Arne Carlson vetoed a $6.7 billion school spending bill. The bill represented the state's contribution to public elementary and secondary education, about 70 percent of the money Minnesotans spend on schools. It accounted for nearly one-third of the state's total spending.

The bill included "90 percent of what the governor wanted," Senate Majority Leader Roger Moe told the press—three extra days of school, more charter schools and lab schools, and a 19 percent increase in state spending on education over two years, including targeted money for struggling schools in the Twin Cities. Not enough, Carlson's veto said. The bill lacked a vital provision, one Carlson wanted desperately—tax credits and tax deductions that would compensate parents for education-related expenses such as educational summer camps, computers, and even private school tuition. That proposal, which was to be the crowning effort of Carlson's work in education, had been bitterly opposed by members of Minnesota's teachers' unions, and by the Democrats who controlled the legislature. The governor was determined to push it through, and 1997 was his last chance.

He was, said one staffer, "taking on the biggest dragon in the woods," when he challenged the teachers' union on this issue. Legislators appeared just as determined to stop him. Representative Mindy Greiling of Roseville remembered one legislator who put it bluntly: "I'm only going to vote for this if it's completely stuck up my ass," he said. Added Greiling, "That's what Arne did."

"It was the best and the worst day of my life," recalled Tim Sullivan, then Carlson's director of strategic planning and the principal architect of the school choice proposal. "I was so proud of him for having the courage, the tenacity, the sheer will, and the commitment to veto the bill. I was also terrified for him—and for us. The stakes don't get any higher."

As the exhausted Carlson staffers gathered around the governor's conference room table in the basement of the Capitol that morning, they considered the possible outcomes of the struggle over the education bill. What would happen if summer passed and there was no education funding, as legislators had threatened? "We're prepared to go all summer," Moe had said. "When fall arrives and a K-12 bill remains in limbo, we'll see how long the Republicans last."

Much more than just a school spending bill or Carlson's desire to find new ways to improve education in Minnesota was on the line on May 21 and in the weeks that followed the veto. Carlson and his staff believed the veto put the remainder of his term in office on the line. Even though he was not planning to run for a third term as governor—and had let everyone know that— Carlson did not want to lose his effectiveness in his final 18 months.

"My biggest fear was that they [legislators] would come back for the special session and pass exactly the same bill," Carlson said. He was prepared to veto it a second time, but he did not believe Republican lawmakers would be able to sustain a second veto. If the veto were overridden, he would have lost his effectiveness as governor as well. "I'd have been limping out of office," Carlson said.

"He was not going to give up," said Susan Heegaard, the governor's liaison with the legislature on education issues. Said Tim Sullivan, "It was a defining moment in his gubernatorial tenure. Probably the defining moment."

But it had been a long time in coming.

AN EVOLUTIONARY CHANGE

Carlson came into office with education as his top priority. Because education had changed the course of his own life so significantly, Carlson had always been interested in and supportive of schools and teachers. Even as state auditor, he talked about education endlessly. On car trips to small towns to present audit reports, Carlson and his secretary Mary Thomas argued about giving vouchers—certificates equivalent to the state's contribution to each child's education—to parents of private school students. She was for them; he opposed them.

In the 1990 election, the Minnesota Education Association—the state's major teachers' union—approached Carlson to offer its endorsement. While the teachers were traditional supporters of Democrats, they grew angry with Governor Rudy Perpich for his support of open enrollment, which allowed public school parents to send their children to the public school of their choice. Their endorsement surprised Carlson, but he felt the teachers appreciated his broad-based approach to education and his focus on preventive programs to help kids. He accepted their endorsement and the 49,000-member union became his campaign's largest financial contributor.

During the budget crisis of 1991, Carlson instructed his staff to prevent as many cuts as possible in education spending, especially for K-12. Still the modest increases the new administration proposed were not enough to satisfy the union. Their criticism of Carlson for limiting the increases in spending "caused a lot of anger in the administration," the governor recalled. "The only solution would have been to go out and raise taxes, which during poor times is one of the dumber things you can do."

Carlson had even appointed former MEA executive director Gene Mammenga as commissioner of education. The funding fight and Mammenga's close ties to the MEA began to limit the commissioner's effectiveness. During the Carlson administration's first year, as it became clear that the governor wouldn't follow the MEA's lead on education issues, the relationship with the union and the commissioner became uncomfortable. The commissioner resigned before the year was out.

The budget battles signaled a growing rift between Carlson and the MEA that never healed. The union expected Carlson to follow its agenda entirely, something he would not do. "Whatever he did, it wasn't enough," one staffer recalled. Said Carlson, "Their agenda is wages, benefits, and shorter hours—the exact opposite of what I thought it was."

In addition to his changing relationship with the teachers, Carlson's views on the effectiveness of Minnesota's schools were also beginning to shift. Carlson began his first term as governor believing that education in Minnesota basically worked—it needed only fine-tuning and more money. Minnesota students performed well against the rest of the nation in college entrance tests and in the number of students going to college. Those indicators measured only how well top students—those heading to college—performed. The rest of the classroom was in trouble. The methods Carlson chose to address the problems, however, evolved as he was in office longer and began to see in action the forces that prevented educational reform.

"The thing that underlies all of the reforms he wanted in education is accountability," said Ann Schluter, a former teacher and school board member who handled education issues for Carlson early in his first term. "The system should be accountable to kids and to society. It really galls him that here we have a system in which, if a kid does not make it through, the system has no responsibility. If a child doesn't succeed because he never truly learned to read, whose fault is that? Accountability was a real motivator for [Carlson]. He'd give speeches on education, and sound so angry. But it wasn't anger, it was passion."

Carlson was determined to improve accountability and to encourage innovation. In 1991, he appointed First Lady Susan Carlson and U S West Chief Executive Officer Ron James cochairs of the Action for Children Commission. A year later, the 25-member, bipartisan commission suggested 36 strategies to improve the lives of Minnesota children, aimed at reducing poverty, providing community support for family, and integrating schools more fully into communities. It recommended the use of 17 children's indicators to measure the status of children in the state. The indicators included everything from the number of children living in poverty to the percentage of children who watch more than 21 hours a week of television. From that commission's work, Carlson promoted a statewide awareness campaign—developed with the help of then-head of the Minnesota Planning Agency Linda Kohl—called Kids Can't Wait to draw attention to prevention programs for children. These reports became the blueprint for many of the Carlson Administration's initiatives with children.

Also in 1991, Carlson signed a law that allowed the establishment of the first charter schools in the nation. Some charter schools focused on arts, sciences, or a new way of teaching. Parents played a significant role in how the school operated. The charter schools became the boutiques of education, designed to offer innovation and specialization to public school students. During his time in office, Carlson and the legislature battled repeatedly over charter schools: How many would be allowed? What regulations would they have to follow? Would they be funded equally with public schools? Despite the opposition, by May 1998, 34 schools were approved for operation in Minnesota—and the number was expected to double in the year after he left office.

Despite the constant budget pressures, state spending per pupil increased by an average of 10 percent a year during the first six years of Carlson's administration. While Carlson continued to believe that Minnesota's basic system worked, he wanted to find ways to improve efficiency.

To that end, in 1993 Carlson pushed another recommendation from the Action for Children Commission—a proposal to merge the state's 250 programs for children into a single agency. During that same year, more than 33 agencies, boards, and commissions spent $4.5 billion trying to address children's issues. "With the very best of intentions, we have created a tangled, bureaucratic web of children's programs," Carlson said at the time. "We have created too many individual government specialty shops. And we invite our customers to wait in line to see if they might be able to squeeze into the narrow product we are selling. If they cannot, they trudge on to the next shop."

It took two years, but the Department of Children, Families, and Learning emerged in 1995. It employed a "cradle-to-career" approach, combining elementary and secondary education programs, many early childhood initiatives, child-focused welfare programs, violence prevention, and assorted grant programs. The cradle-to-career approach included the addition of a School-to-Work Initiative, which prepared students for jobs through 19 state-funded youth apprenticeships and 50 privately supported school-to-work projects. Carlson also promoted a similar efficiency move for the state-run colleges and universities. In 1991, he merged the state's community colleges, state universities, and technical schools into a single system.

While Minnesota's educational system was excellent in many ways, it did not produce positive results for all children. In 1996, the state hired an independent company to test students in basic skills. The results shocked the governor. The testers found that in metropolitan school districts 53 percent of high school students performed below the basic level of skill— an eighth-grade level—in math, and 62 percent performed below the basic level in reading. That same year, 39 percent of eighth graders scored at a level considered "below basic" on a National Assessment of Educational Progress math test.

"When so many children cannot perform at basic levels in math and reading, it is clear that we have failed them," Carlson said.

THE 'V' WORD

By 1996, Carlson was ready to attempt a discussion of school choice. The idea of using vouchers to increase parents' choices for their children's schooling had been around for many years, advocated mostly by parochial schools and their supporters. The idea also had been promoted by former U.S. Representative Vin Weber and University of Minnesota Professor John Brandl in their report on the ways state government could prepare Minnesotans for the future.

Vouchers had no popular support, however. Many conservatives believed that vouchers would be the first step toward more government control of private schools. Representative Steve Sviggum, the Republican minority leader in the house and a staunch Carlson ally most of the time, attacked the idea vigorously. Carlson felt that at least a discussion of vouchers might push public schools toward more competitiveness and greater accountability. He wanted schools to start looking more seriously at how they could improve outcomes—that is, how much students actually learned.

Carlson staffer Bernie Omann remembered how Carlson would put his hand at his throat and say, "The word is right here. I'm almost ready to say it."

The word was vouchers.

Carlson knew he would lose any voucher fight in the legislature. Winning was not a goal in 1996. He wanted debate. The governor proposed vouchers on an experimental basis in four school districts, including Minneapolis and St. Paul. Few legislators supported the idea, and the teachers' union went ballistic.

"I liked the idea of vouchers," Carlson said, "but I knew it would never pass. I wanted to sell the idea of competition. We wanted the debate. What the debate revealed was that the opposition had no answers. Nobody could fight us on outcomes."

Carlson's voucher proposal never made it out of committee in 1996. (It got only one positive vote, from Representative Leroy Koppendrayer, a Republican from Princeton.) But public opinion polls showed him that voters were more open to the idea of vouchers than legislators. A Gallup Poll taken in 1996 found that 36 percent of Americans supported vouchers, a huge increase from the 24 percent who had supported the idea three years earlier. While Carlson was trounced in the legislature on the issue, his efforts impressed presidential candidate Bob Dole, who came to Minnesota to announce his own voucher plan.

A BETTER IDEA

Carlson took some hard-earned lessons away from the 1996 voucher fight. First, he discovered that Minnesotans were uncomfortable with the V-word. If the same idea were called a "scholarship program" or an "education certificate" parents were more likely to support it. Finally, he learned that parents must understand clearly how the program would benefit them. He also knew he would have to build a large grassroots coalition to push educational reform. This fight he could not win alone. Each of those lessons changed how he approached educational reform in 1997.

In the summer of 1996, Carlson told Tim Sullivan he wanted three things. He wanted a new plan for school choice. He wanted a coalition to support it. Finally, he wanted to win this time. It was a daunting task the governor laid before Sullivan and several other staffers including Omann, Todd Johnson, Heegaard, and David Leckey. "It was up to us to come up with the plan, the coalition, and the win," Sullivan recalled. "Lots of people were coming to me saying 'You're being set up for failure. This just won't happen.' When we looked at the political environment, we realized that we didn't have a single advantage in our corner, other than a committed governor."

They first developed the outline of a plan. For any proposal to have a chance at winning, it needed to appeal to a broader group of people than vouchers did. "It had to invest the middle class," Sullivan said. "It couldn't be just for poor kids in the city. It had to invest public school parents. Lastly, it had to address the core concerns of the Republican base."

A system of credits and deductions for educational expenses seemed to fit the bill. The group determined that only expenses that research demonstrated improved school performance could be deducted. These included expenses like hiring a tutor, buying a computer for home, or sending a child to summer school. Tuition for private education also counted.

"We merged the political assessment [of what might be passed] with what we thought was very strong research," said Sullivan, a high-energy intellectual with the lean look of a marathon runner. "It allowed us to argue the issue in a whole different way. Now we were talking about a tax break for every single Minnesota parent. It changed the issue from public versus private schools to parents versus the status quo."

Lastly, the proposal had to be lawsuit proof. The state already allowed the tax deductions on a limited basis, preventing a court challenge. Carlson knew at once that this was a better direction. "We were frozen on the destination, not the vehicle," Carlson said.

He was so enthusiastic about the idea when staffers first presented him with it in August 1996 that Carlson wanted to immediately announce the plan. His staff argued against that, saying that bringing the issue out before the 1996 elections would force too many legislators to promise teachers that they would oppose this new plan. So Carlson held his fire, and his staff began building a climate in which the proposal could pass.

Starting in the summer, Carlson talked about school performance everywhere he went, and he traveled all across the state. Minnesotans have a deep well of good feeling toward their schools, just as Carlson had when he first was elected. Voters needed to understand that problems existed in the schools before they would accept a proposal as radical as the one Carlson had in mind.

Carlson also needed a network of people to promote and support school choice. One of the first people his staff contacted was Kristin Robins, newly appointed executive director of Minnesotans for School Choice. Robins' group pulled together a variety of people who stood to benefit from greater educational choice, including Catholic school parents, parents who taught their children at home, and Lutheran and Evangelical school supporters. She also worked with the Minnesota Family Council, which provided a newspaper to carry stories of the effort to more than 100,000 people. The school choice group sent mail to its supporters, urged letter-writing campaigns, and encouraged supporters to let legislators know that parents needed more choice in education.

The second prong of the coalition involved business groups—organizations that usually stayed out of educational issues. This time, urged by the governor and distressed at the low levels of academic achievement of many entry-level workers, business got on board.

"The business piece was very important," Robins said, "because legislators know that business had never been mobilized around this issue."

By the time Carlson unveiled his plan in December 1996, more than 30 organizations supported him. Despite overtures from the governor's office, representatives of minority groups had not joined the coalition, a disappointment for Carlson who felt minority children suffered most in poor schools. As a result of his relentless speechmaking on the problems in education, support for school choice among the general public had grown. In February, a poll commissioned by Robins' group found that 65 percent of Minnesotans liked the idea of tax credits and deductions for parents to spend on education. An astonishing 78 percent also supported the idea of statewide testing, a key element in Carlson's plan.

Carlson won the testing fight on May 12, when he signed the bill removing the statewide ban on standardized testing and providing uniform statewide testing in grades three, five, eight, and once during high school. The class of 2002 would be the first to make it to graduation under the tough new standards.

It was a major step toward accountability, because statewide testing set the backdrop for competition. The test scores gave parents some leverage to improve their children's education. At last, parents could compare school performance in an objective way. "The key to everything was test scores," Carlson said. "Ultimately the market would change and say that what we have now is not acceptable. Once you cross that bridge, it's not hard to go the rest of the way."

While testing had passed, the governor's plan to provide $150 million in tax credits and deductions to parents who home-school their children—or who spend money on private school tuition, computers and educational software, educational summer camps, tutors, and other educational services—was in trouble. Despite the encouraging polls, legislators could not swallow this idea because of the vehement opposition of teachers' unions. When the final education bill passed the House and Senate, the tax credit and deduction proposal had been deleted.

Carlson vetoed the bill.

In the governor's conference room the day after the K-12 school-spending veto, the Carlson team pulled itself together. The group included Sullivan, Heegaard, Carlson's Chief of Staff Morrie Anderson, Deputy Chief Bernie Omann, Press Secretary Brian Dietz, and Legal Counsel Tanja Kozicky. Carlson's calmly determined demeanor quieted fears, and the task of assembling an action plan for a special legislative session channeled nervous energy as Carlson's team considered possible legislative responses and how those might play out.

"The difficulty of this experience cannot be underestimated," Carlson said. "I can honestly say that the month following the veto of the education bill was one of the most difficult months of my life."

Avoiding a shutdown of the schools was a high priority. But if the governor's special-session initiative lost, schools would be the foremost issue in the upcoming election. Carlson's greatest fear was that the legislature would return for the special session and pass exactly the bill he had vetoed. Then the question would be whether the administration could hold its Republican votes in place to sustain a second veto. Minority Leader Sviggum, who so vigorously opposed vouchers, liked the tax credit and deduction plan. He promised the governor he would hold the Republicans together, making a veto override impossible. Still, the pressure on Republican lawmakers would be intense.

Nevertheless, Carlson made up his mind early in the days following his veto of the 1997 K-12 spending bill that, should the legislature pass essentially the same bill again, he would veto it again. One thing Carlson had going for him at that point was his noncandidacy. The legislators would be facing the voters in 1998. He would never face them again.

'You have nothing to lose unless you own something," Carlson said. "They owned the 1998 election. I didn't."

GOING TO THE COMMUNITIES

One way to ensure Carlson could endure another veto was to increase public pressure on legislators. If Carlson's supporters could energize the public, legislators could be persuaded. A last-minute radio and television advertising campaign, funded by the Choice in Education League of Minnesota, at the end of the session had surprised opponents. A similar campaign was planned for just before the special session with Kristin Robins directing the effort. They wanted to expand the school choice coalition as much as possible.

About a month earlier, Carlson's legal counsel Tanja Kozicky had brought up the idea of going back to the minority communities for support. Sullivan felt this was a risky tactic because it had the potential to backfire. Minorities had always been the most loyal Democratic voters in the electorate. If they remained silent on school choice, it did not hurt Carlson. However, if groups representing minorities announced their opposition, it could kill the school choice idea. "We'd sit and talk about how 60 percent of minorities didn't pass [the achievement tests], but we hadn't really heard from these communities," Kozicky said. "Why weren't test scores making people morally outraged?"

After intense internal debate, Carlson gave Kozicky permission to try again with minorities, this time by going through the state-appointed councils on minority affairs. The state had four councils—Indian Affairs, Chicano-Latino Affairs, Black Minnesotans, and Asian and Pacific Islanders. Kozicky made an ideal emissary. An elegant, soft-spoken lawyer, she is the granddaughter of Hispanic migrant workers who came to Minnesota to pick sugar beets. By the time her mother was 5, both parents had died. Despite being shuffled from foster homes to orphanages, Kozicky's mother graduated from high school and was offered a scholarship to college.

"It really struck a chord with me," Kozicky said. "Could I have been one of those kids failing in a center city school if I had not grown up in a suburb?"

Her first appointment was with the Council on Black Minnesotans. This proved a good place to start. Dolores Fridge, Carlson's commissioner of human rights, chaired the council and behind the scenes she had been talking with council members about endorsing Carlson's school choice proposal. Kozicky went to the Martin Luther King Center in St. Paul to make the pitch. The Council had assembled a group of 25 leaders from across the African-American community to listen and ask questions. With the cool logic of her law school training, Kozicky laid out the test scores and the funding figures for education. We've spent lots of money on public schools, she told the council members, and your children are failing.

"I said, 'There's no time for niceties. There's no time to talk about improving motivation. Now's the time to create opportunity for your kids,'" Kozicky recalled. Community leaders discussed proposed reforms for over four hours. Eventually, they issued a report that endorsed Carlson's tax-credit proposal. Kozicky—and other Carlson staffers—were thrilled, but their goal had always been to have one press conference with members of all of the councils of color. Her next target was the Hispanic community.

Without an advocate like Fridge on the Chicano-Latino Affairs Council, Kozicky decided to try another avenue into the Hispanic community. For many years, Carlson had been supportive of the work done by the Our Lady of Guadalupe Catholic Church in St. Paul. With assistance from Alberto Quintela, an aide to St. Paul Mayor Norm Coleman, Kozicky went to see the Reverend Hugo Montero, pastor of Our Lady of Guadalupe. On a Friday afternoon, Kozicky and Quintela stopped at the church and asked the priest if he would allow Carlson to address the congregation on school choice. Montero agreed and said Carlson could speak that Sunday afternoon—June 8. "I was stunned," recalled Kozicky.

The day dawned warm, and by afternoon, the packed church was sweltering hot. Carlson spoke for over an hour—telling the story of his own educational journey and outlining why he thought parents needed more choices. For a long time, he took questions from members of the parish. Support for the plan ran deep, especially the amount of control it gave parents. Hundreds of parents signed a petition in support of the plan that day. Afterwards, Carmen Robles, a long-time supporter in the Hispanic community garnered more signatures and mailed the petitions to legislators. George Perez, president of the Hispanic Bar Association, coordinated an outreach plan to Hispanic business and community leaders.

"When the governor went to Our Lady of Guadalupe, that's when the Democrats took notice," Kozicky said. The meeting at the church seemed to clinch the endorsement of the Chicano-Latino Affairs Council as well.

At the same time Carlson and his staff reached out to the minority community, the governor decided to get personal on this issue. He felt that many politicians in Minnesota and the nation behaved hypocritically about education. They sang the praises of public education and courted the teachers' unions, but sent their own children to private schools. As the special session neared, Carlson resolved to go public with the names of opposition legislators who sent their children to private schools.

Carlson said later, "To me, it's hypocritical. Why is this system [school choice] good for your children and not good for other children? If they're going to get up on the House floor and lead the fight against choice, they have to explain why their kids go to private school."

The administration singled out three DFL representatives—Darlene Luther, Ted Winter, and Carlos Mariani—who sent their children to private schools while fighting the plan to give low- and moderate-income parents tax credits to do the same. The attacks hurt. "I don't know what the governor is trying to prove by all this," retorted Mariani in the press. "I wish he would get back on track and focus on what the real issue is, instead of personalizing a very important real political debate."

As the clock ticked toward the special session, Carlson and DFL leaders met periodically to discuss possible compromises.

None of them directly asked Carlson if he would veto a second time. "We were like dogs," Carlson said. "They were smelling me more than asking me to see what I might do."

But the negotiators seemed to be at an impasse. "Even if we limited it to Minneapolis and St. Paul, we'd be asking other school districts to take a cut so that some parents in the Twin Cities could send their children to private schools. That's not acceptable," said Speaker of the House Phil Carruthers.

"Governor Carlson can order us into special session, but once we're here, we control what happens," Moe told reporters.

Carlson continued negotiating with Moe, Carruthers, and other DFLers before the special session. Representatives Becky Kelso, Joe Opatz, and Leroy Koppendrayer often acted as messengers, carrying the plans back and forth among the negotiators. It seemed they would never reach agreement. Any help for parents of private school students was unacceptable to the Democrats, and Carlson was just as adamant that the bill must include his tax credit and deduction plan. "It's kind of difficult to negotiate when you're being told it's nonnegotiable," Carruthers complained to the press.

At one negotiating session, Dolores Fridge spoke. A tall, black woman with a commanding voice, Fridge riveted legislators with a story. She told about a mother whose husband was fighting in the Vietnam War while she worked as a Minneapolis public school teacher. Despite the family's sacrifices, their daughter could not seem to succeed in public schools. The child was intelligent, her mother felt, but in the wrong environment. The school insisted she needed special education. Finally, the mother approached her father about lending her the money for private school tuition. In a different environment, the child flourished.

"Just so you're clear about this," Fridge told the legislators, "the woman in that story is me."

"Our kids are not dumb, but they get dumber everyday attending public schools," Fridge said. It was hard for her and other African-Americans to appear to be attacking teachers, Fridge said, because teaching had been a profession that welcomed blacks with college degrees. But the time to stand up for the kids had come.

Said Carlson, "When Dolores Fridge is on an issue, look out. It's like a tank coming at you. Those legislators didn't stand a chance."

On June 12, the press conference Carlson and his staff had wanted occurred. Carlson appeared with members of the state Council on Black Minnesotans and the Chicano-Latino Affairs Council who offered their official endorsement of his school choice plan. The Council for Asians and Pacific Islanders never took a formal vote on the plan, but several members and other leaders in the Asian community attended the press conference to support it. The Indian Affairs council did not participate.

"Our tax credit program will directly help thousands of minority students who are disproportionately failing in our existing system," Carlson told the media that day. "Our program will provide these Minnesota families with much needed resources to take advantage of educational choices that will best serve their individual needs."

Chicano-Latino Affairs Council member Juan Martinez said, "The governor's plan will extend real choices to our community and will open up a system that traditionally has not served our children well."

A picture from the news conference appeared in the Minneapolis paper the next day, and Carlson could sense almost palpably the wilting of the opposition. "We knew at this point we had them on the defensive," Carlson said later. "They could only play defense."

Mariani, a vigorous opponent of Carlson's plan, admitted to the *Star Tribune*, "The governor has tapped into some very real things here. To the extent that there is a failure in the public school system, it's with low-income and minority students. I've told my DFL caucus that the Achilles heel of public education is minority kids."

At the same time, school choice advocates unleashed a $300,000 media campaign, going directly to the public seeking support for the plan. Legislators took notice. After rallying minority support and going public with the names of legislators who opposed choice but who sent their kids to private schools, negotiations to work out a K-12 spending bill were reasonably polite; but the sticking point over whether tuition would be allowed in the tax credit for low- and moderate-income families remained.

Legislators Koppendrayer, Opatz, and Kelso had been working for some time to come up with a plan that allowed a credit for tuition without actually calling it "tuition." It was Koppendrayer who first suggested that the plan allow a credit for expenses for "instructional materials." Broadly defined, this could include expenses for books, transportation, and computers in the school. It was in essence "tuition by another name," Sullivan said.

Roger Moe also offered a more generous working-family tax credit (in a companion tax bill being considered at the same time) for lower-income families as a compromise. Carlson could hardly contain his glee. Republicans routinely hate greater tax credits. Carlson loved this one because it included more low-income families under his school-choice umbrella.

Before one of the final negotiating sessions, Carlson, Robins, Sullivan, Kozicky, and several others met in the office of Bernie Omann, upstairs from the conference room where the governor and legislators were meeting. Everyone in the room liked the instructional materials idea, but Carlson was not sure it would work.

"He was so committed. We had to convince him this would work," Robins recalled.

Finally, Carlson aide Todd Johnson—whose children attended a small religious school—told the governor he was convinced schools could separate the expense easily enough that parents would be able to take advantage of the credit. That sealed the deal.

On June 26, both houses of the legislature passed the bill overwhelmingly. The lopsided victory came in part because of last-minute lobbying by the state's teachers' unions that offended some legislators. "I think they [legislators] were angry when teachers made it seem like the Democrats had caved to the governor," Sullivan said. "It made them feel like the teachers' union was unpleaseable, completely unreasonable in their demands. Legislators know how to cut a deal with the governor. The teachers' union did not."

Representative Becky Kelso said, "All special interest groups are in many ways purists. I would hope that they would have seen the effects would be far worse if this had not been settled."

The bill gave Carlson everything he wanted. The legislation included money for charter and lab schools, technological upgrades, statewide testing, three extra school days, site-based management, and aid for schools that serve disadvantaged students. It also called for a higher deduction for private-school tuition and for expanding tax deductions to cover computers and software, tutoring, educational summer camps, and "instruction materials" at private schools.

The bill raised the deduction from $650 to $1,625 for students in grades K-6 and from $1,000 to $2,500 for those in grades 7-12. It boosted the Working Family Credit by 25 percent, returning money to families earning $29,000 or less annually. The average increase amounted to $200 to $350 per family.

Finally, the bill created a tax credit of up to $2,000 that families with incomes up to $33,500 could apply to educational camps, school transportation, textbooks, and a variety of other expenses.

LEADING THE NATION

With the bill's passage, Minnesota suddenly became the nation's leader in school choice. In an editorial following the Minnesota vote, the *Wall Street Journal* began, "Education reformers of the world take heart." The editorial lauded the Minnesota plan and said that "both the new law and the way he [Carlson] made it happen could become a model for the country." On a subsequent visit to Washington, D.C., Carlson met with congressional leaders and gave speeches to the National Press Club and the Heritage Foundation. Said Sullivan, "It was a D.C. schedule that would be the envy of any presidential candidate."

After that, Carlson was asked to contribute to books on educational reform and to speak on the issue from New Hampshire to California. More importantly, the Minnesota model served as the framework for national legislation to allow greater school choice

In February 1998, while attending a White House gathering for the nation's governors, Carlson even criticized the "Washington establishment" that "sends its kids to private schools and at the same time tells parents of other children that they have no choice."

His tough approach may be what's necessary to make changes in the educational establishment. "Every governor who wants to make progress in education is going to have to spend some time raising tough questions about what's going on in the system," said Joe Nathan, a nationally recognized expert on schools based at the University of Minnesota. "Even though he'll be accused of teacher bashing."

"Schools are being ranked," said Bob Wedl, commissioner of the Department of Children, Families, and Learning. "People can see who is doing a good job and who isn't."

Even the MEA agreed that Carlson had a positive impact. The most important Carlson legacy in education was the graduation standards, agreed MEA President Judy Schaubach at the end of the Carlson years.

Said Nathan, "He took a state that was pretty complacent and said, 'Lets take a look at what's really going on.' This was a real shock to the system."

After his school choice victory, Carlson still had some unfinished business in education. In 1998, he proposed—and got—the first residential academies for state-funded boarding schools for at-risk youth. The initiatives stemmed from both his own experiences and from what his wife, Susan, saw daily as a district court referee. Carlson observers said that the kid from Bronx looked at Minnesota dropouts and thought, "There but for the grace of God go I."

Carlson the hardball politician knew his own background lent him just the political leverage he needed to win education reform in Minnesota to the extent that he did. Carlson agreed with both estimations. "Education for me closed the circle," he said. "It allowed me to get back in contact with my own child-hood. If I had been wealthy I could not have done it. It's very hard to debate with a person who has gone from being poor to attending a very well-accepted school, with that level of experi-ence and commitment. What are they going to say?"

CHAPTER THIRTEEN

JUDGES AND JUSTICE

Carlson Creates a Lasting Legacy in Minnesota Courts

Shortly after Kathleen Blatz left the Minnesota Legislature to become a Hennepin County District Court judge, she received a telephone call from her long-time friend and political ally, Governor Arne Carlson. The governor, who sounded upset, had just heard about a 12-year-old runaway who was being forced to return home to an abusive father. Carlson said that the boy had told social workers his dad was beating him up, but the courts kept sending him back to his parents anyway.

"The governor demanded to know, 'What is going on? How can this possibly happen?'" Blatz later recalled.

Not long after that conversation, at Carlson's request, Blatz convened a group of judges, county attorneys, children's guardians *ad litem*, and several other people who were known to be concerned about children's issues to discuss the workings of juvenile court. "One of the group's most important conclusions was that we had to open up the juvenile courts," Blatz said. "So, the governor just wanted to get it done."

Eventually, a court-appointed task force recommended that juvenile court hearings be opened to the public and the media.

When Blatz was sworn in as chief justice of Minnesota's Supreme Court in 1998, one of the first things she did in her new role was to act on that recommendation by announcing her first major initiative—a pilot program that would open the juvenile courts for a three-year trial period.

It was a controversial move, albeit one that some people considered gutsy, and several of Blatz's colleagues immediately cautioned her about it. One person who did not caution Blatz, however, was Arne Carlson. The governor wanted a gutsy chief justice who was willing to push for change in the courts.

In Kathleen Blatz, Carlson saw a person he considered exceptionally well qualified to lead the Minnesota court system into the next century. Not yet 50, she had experience in the legislature, on the district bench, and in the Supreme Court. She also had a vision of how to surmount both the challenges facing today's courts and those that society would present to the courts in the future.

The selection and appointment of judges may provide a governor's most lasting legacy, one whose influence will be felt long after his or her administration and its policies have faded into history, and long after future legislatures have modified or rescinded the bills that the governor signed into law. Although Blatz was Carlson's most publicized judicial appointee, his criteria for choosing her exemplified his general approach to selecting the people he would appoint to the bench.

Regarding the part of a judge's job that involves interpreting the law, Carlson was always looking for "a moderate or strict constructionist," according to Supreme Court Justice James H. Gilbert, who led Carlson's Judicial Merit Selection Commission for five years. "On the procedures, though, on how the courts function and how they are managed, he was always looking for creative change." If all the other departments and branches of government, as well as private industry, were making changes to keep up with the changing times, then the courts were going to have to make procedural changes too.

By the end of his second term, Carlson had appointed close to 90 district court judges—approximately a third of the 254-member court. He also appointed eight people to the 16-member Court of Appeals and six people to the 7-member Supreme Court, as well as five Workers' Compensation Court of Appeals judges, five Tax Court judges, and one chief judge to the office of administrative hearings.

Republicans and Democrats alike praised Carlson's appointments to the bench. "I think that the people Governor Carlson selected are really good people. I think he's done a good job, and I'm normally critical of the governor," said state Representative Wes Skoglund, a Minneapolis DFLer who served in the House for 21 years and chaired the Judiciary Committee for 5 years. "That part of his legacy is good; people have been well served by his appointments."

Carlson has gone outside the ranks of Republican Party activists to find qualified lawyers, said Mark Gehan, president of the Minnesota State Bar Association, "I think that most people are generally pretty satisfied with his appointments. I also think that the commission does a good job at getting him a qualified group of people," Gehan said.

THE FIRST LADY FOR CHILDREN

Justice Joan Ericksen Lancaster remembered the excitement at the Hennepin County Courthouse when the judges and staff found out about the new referee coming in to hear detention cases. Detention may be the least glamorous job in the court system, but the new referee had a bona fide claim to celebrity.

"It was exciting to have someone here who is a big deal,"

Lancaster said of Susan Carlson, Minnesota's first lady, and a lawyer by training. "But when we met her, she was so down-to-earth, so hardworking, and so unfailingly pleasant, that everyone just fell in love with her."

Susan Carlson's job in the courts gave Governor Carlson a rare perspective on the impact of the justice system on children. Her work also led to landmark

Carlson always placed a high priority on the selection of judges, and many of his appointments were "firsts." For example, Carlson was the first and only Minnesota governor to take the time to interview every finalist for district court appointments. Also, Carlson had the distinction of appointing the first female chief justice of the Supreme Court. He also appointed the first woman to lead the Court of Appeals and subsequently appointed the first African American as chief judge of that court. And, he appointed more women to the court than any other governor in history.

But beyond the "firsts" are other important aspects of Carlson's impact on the court. He wanted to depoliticize the process of selecting judges, and he enforced the use of the Judicial Merit Selection Commission to make sure it happened. His success in depoliticizing the court was such that Justice Sandra Gardebring, a staunch Democrat and Perpich appointee, gave up her seat on the court in the summer of 1998, saying she had been so impressed by Carlson's appointments that she saw no need to wait to retire in case a Democrat won the 1998 guber-

legislation to help children with fetal alcohol syndrome. Susan Carlson began working as a rotating referee in Hennepin County in 1995. She often heard detention cases, but also was assigned to juvenile court and family court. After several months on the bench, she began to see a pattern among her cases.

"I'd see 10 or 15 cases in the morning and fewer than that in the afternoon," Susan said. "You look through these thick case files and the psychological profiles were so similar. The children came from families where substance abuse was a problem and they had the same mental health and behavior problems. After a while, I thought, there's a connection here."

The youngsters who appeared again and again in Carlson's courtroom suffered from attention deficit disorder, hyperactivity, poor school performance, and serious mental health concerns. Many suffered from low intelligence and natorial election. Carlson also wanted to find people who were willing to change the system and to advocate for young people. From the very beginning of his governorship, Carlson stressed that a primary goal of his administration would be to focus on what he called the prevention agenda. This included an array of policy initiatives and procedural changes to prevent future social problems by helping children grow up healthy, safe, and well educated.

"The court was to be a part of that," Carlson said. When he first came into office, the courts had already made some creative changes, so what was needed was the provision of a stronger impetus for the prevention agenda—in some organized fashion.

"Children have a right to expect of [parents] a high degree of protection. And that relationship involves an enormous amount of trust. Now, when a parent beats the daylights out of a child, it's pretty obvious that relationship is being sorely abused. The question then becomes 'What responsibility do the rest of us have to have?' We have a responsibility to the child. Our society now protects the adult, not the child," Carlson said. "That's what Blatz

even those with normal or above average intelligence appeared to have difficulty understanding the consequences of their actions. All of the symptoms pointed to a common disorder, fetal alcohol syndrome (FAS).

A computer buff, Carlson spent weekends at home cruising the Internet for information about fetal alcohol syndrome and its effects. What she found was frightening. Minnesota ranked fourth highest nationally in frequent drinking by women of child-bearing age, potentially exposing thousands of unborn babies to damage. Even one binge-drinking episode during a pregnancy could lead to FAS or Fetal Alcohol Effect, the leading cause of mental retardation nationally. The disease is not always apparent to doctors immediately after birth. Its effects show themselves over time and they do not improve.

"Susan was the first person on the bench to observe this pattern," is going to turn around."

According to former Minnesota Supreme Court Chief Justice A. M. "Sandy" Keith, Carlson "has a strong commitment to young people. He is concerned. He realizes that you can't incarcerate yourself into safety. That you can't just put everybody in prison. That we've got to work on our young people. I think he's looking for leaders in the legislature, the judiciary, and the executive branch—for people who are committed to trying to deal with these social issues, especially [with regard to] young people at a very early age."

Keith credited Carlson with several accomplishments. First, he focused on preventing social problems. "On social issues, Governor Carlson certainly has a broad view and a view that the majority basically has in this state," Keith said. The governor also appointed significant numbers of women to the bench, so that the judiciary at the end of Carlson's second term reflected more closely the state's population of attorneys. Finally, the governor was much less partisan than previous administrations, particularly in choosing judges for the district courts.

Lancaster said. "Once she pointed it out, I started to see it too."

Alarmed at what she was seeing in the courtroom and what her research showed her, Susan urged her husband to get the state involved in preventing FAS. In 1997, Susan spearheaded a proposal to the legislature for $4 million in funding for FAS-prevention education and a proposal to allow involuntary commitment of pregnant women who could not or would not control their drinking. The controversial proposal stemmed from the frequency of FAS within families.

"I have seen women with three, four, five, or six children, all of whom have FAS," Susan told reporters when she introduced the proposal. "This gives us a tool—I'll call it tough love—to bring people in when they can't control themselves."

The legislature funded just $1.75 million of the request. In July 1997, Governor Carlson appointed a

"I think the vast majority of his appointments have really been people who want to do a good job and work hard," Keith said.

SHAPING THE APPELLATE COURTS

From his first day in office, Carlson knew that his key appointment was going to be the chief justice of the Supreme Court. He also knew that to fill the appointment, he wanted to find a person who not only understood emerging issues, such as high divorce rates, high rates of family breakdown, and increased violence coupled with decreased age of violence, but also would take the court in the direction of the prevention agenda.

"Kathleen Blatz was an ideal fit because during her whole career—as a social worker, as an attorney, and as a judge—she had dealt with these emerging issues. So, she was a natural," Carlson said. "Plus, she has leadership ability and very strong people skills that enable her to accomplish whatever she wants to accomplish."

While appointing a new chief justice was vital, Carlson also had a plan for the appellate courts. He contemplated each appoint-

high-profile, 44-member task force, co-chaired by Susan Carlson and Judge Lancaster, to study FAS and make recommendations to the state.

The cochairs took the FAS Task Force on the road. They held nine hearings around the state to gather information from local communities. The group came back to the legislature in 1998 with another proposal, this time for $5 million in funding for FAS. Said Christina Rich, the Carlson legislative liaison who worked with Susan on the bill, "Her level of interest and involvement was incredibly detailed and deep. She wanted to be at the Capitol everyday. She knew her presence would add to the significance of the bill."

Carlson testified before nearly every committee the FAS legislation passed through. While being the wife of the governor made it easier for Carlson to get the attention of legislators, it was ment with an eye toward balancing each court with the different skills and disciplines it needed.

"When we put Anne Simonett on the district court bench, it was with a clear view that she would ultimately end up on the appellate court, and very likely on the Supreme Court. Likewise Blatz," Carlson said.

Carlson's first two appointments to the Supreme Court came in 1994 when he selected Ed Stringer and Paul Anderson for that bench. Kathleen Blatz was chosen to fill a seat left vacant when Justice M. Jeanne Coyne retired. James Gilbert took Blatz's seat when she replaced Keith as chief justice in 1998. When Justice Esther Tomljanovich announced her retirement in 1998, Carlson selected an experienced district court judge, Russell Anderson, to replace her. Finally, with Justice Sandra Gardebring's departure, Carlson appointed former Hennepin County Judge Joan Ericksen Lancaster to the high court in July 1998.

Keith recalled that while he served as chief justice, Carlson never asked his opinion on whom to appoint. But he did ask

her experience in the court system that gave her credibility.

She often told the story of a 13-year-old she called Tommy. The boy came before her on a shoplifting charge. His mother was a heavy drinker, who abandoned him by the time he was 3. She died later from her alcoholism. Tommy had been in 13 foster homes by the time Carlson saw him. He was a dropout and a ward of the state. Despite relatively high intelligence, Tommy did not understand the consequences of his actions. As a referee, Carlson had to determine a punishment and a new foster home placement for Tommy. But there was little else she could offer him.

"His story is repeated over and over in juvenile court," she said. "And it is 100 percent preventable."

In 1998, the legislature fully funded the $5 million FAS proposal, which included the Birth-to-Three Project. The project,

Keith what types of skills the court needed. Each of Carlson's appointees brought the court an important skill.

Justice Stringer brought a strong corporate background, strong people skills, and a traditional approach that protects and respects the past. Justice Paul Anderson showed a high regard for the emerging issues and the history and majesty of the bench, as well as a keen understanding of the independence of the judicial system. Justice Gilbert filled the need for a heavyweight litigator. And, Chief Justice Blatz brought an innovative approach and an ability to identify with children and to anticipate the emerging issues. Justice Russell Anderson brought the court trial experience and the sensibility of a rural district judge. Justice Lancaster would bring great experience in issues relating to children and social programs.

Not all of Carlson's appointments worked out as planned. In June 1994, he appointed Anne Simonett to the Court of Appeal's chief judge position. A Harvard graduate and concert-level pianist in her youth, Simonett was brilliant and had all of the

begun in July 1998, targeted the highest-risk mothers for FAS births, specifically mothers who already had one FAS child. The mothers received intensive one-to-one services to avoid future FAS births. The bill included funding for regional diagnostic clinics throughout the state to standardize the diagnosis of FAS and to ensure greater access to resources for affected families. It also encouraged voluntary reporting of pregnant women who abused alcohol.

Carlson's work on FAS earned her national recognition, including a leadership award from the National Association for Fetal Alcohol Syndrome presented to her in June 1998. Susan planned to remain involved in the issue after Arne Carlson left the governorship. She formed MOFAS, the first—and only—statewide nonprofit organization dedicated to fighting FAS. "It's really become a lifelong commitment for her," Rich said. ∎

skills the governor wanted for the Court of Appeals. Tragically, a brain tumor forced her resignation less than a year later. Her death at age 42 was a personal loss for Carlson.

"That was a very difficult death to understand," the governor said. "It felt so unfair."

Following Simonett's untimely death, Carlson appointed Edward Toussaint Jr. to fill her seat on the bench. The governor appraised Toussaint's skill as follows: "Ed Toussaint has been a giant in the courtroom. He is very much into the prevention agenda; he knows how to train younger judges coming into the system; he's a bridge builder. He will go down as one of the giants."

Age was an obvious factor in Carlson's appointment strategy. As former Chief Justice Keith noted, "Four of the six [Supreme Court appointments] are extremely young and could be there close to 20 years, which will have an enormous impact on the future of the development of the law in Minnesota."

A strong believer in the idea that each generation has its time on the stage, Carlson wanted to turn the courts over to another generation.

"I think age is terribly important," he said. "You want people who know how to relate. A person of my generation ought not to kid himself that he understands today's 22-year-old. I don't. I don't understand the young people with tattoos. I don't understand teenagers with earrings. You need somebody who's younger and more relevant to that age group. Kathy Blatz is only in her 40s. She's much more connected to it than I am."

MERIT SELECTION ON THE DISTRICT COURT

On April 11, 1991, Governor Arne Carlson stood before a crowded room to announce his first judicial appointments. That day, as he appointed Michael Monahan to the Second Judicial District bench and Catherine Anderson to the Fourth, he also set in motion the judicial selection process that would garner praise throughout his two terms in office.

Carlson's words that April day reflected the honor and sense of duty he brought to his role, his commitment to the recently established merit selection process, and his goals for the judiciary.

"The legislature made very significant judicial reforms, and we want to make sure our administration not only adheres to the letter of the law, but, much more importantly, to the spirit of the law," Carlson said. "The focus of our administration will be on competency and balance."

As he would continue to do for each district court appointment over the next eight years, Carlson selected the judicial appointees from the list of finalists supplied by the Merit Selection Commission. "Each of these appointees cleared the process. We did not skirt the process or go around it, and we did not jump over it," he stressed. "The lieutenant governor and I worked from the list that was given to us. We felt very strongly that we wanted to make sure our approach was totally and completely professional."

Although the statute allowed a governor to disregard the commission's recommendations, Carlson only once chose to exercise that option. "If somebody didn't make it through the judicial selection process, they had no chance of getting appointed," Gilbert said. "In the past, some governors had informal judicial selection commissions and a lot of times their recommendations were discarded.

"Governor Carlson wanted to set some new standards in appointing judges," Gilbert continued. "He wanted to professionalize the appointment process, and depoliticize it too. In the past, over the decades, judgeships sometimes have been patronage jobs. Governor Carlson set the ground rules from day one that candidates had to be good lawyers, that they had to have high integrity, and that they better have already given something back to their communities."

Unlike federal judges, Minnesota judges must stand for election. Every six years, Supreme Court, appellate court, and district court judges must be approved by the voters. Gubernatorial appointments occur when a justice leaves office in midterm. When judges serve out their terms but don't file for reelection, Minnesota voters fill the empty judicial seats in an election.

Under the terms of the statute passed in 1990, a commission on judicial selection must be used to help fill any district court vacancy that occurs midterm. The commission consists of nine at-large members who address all district court judicial vacancies in the state, and four district members in each of the state's 10 judicial districts. So, 13 commission members participate in the selection process for each vacancy, including nine members appointed by the governor and four members appointed by the Minnesota Supreme Court.

When a midterm opening occurred on the district court bench, the Merit Selection Commission recruited and evaluated candidates. It then recommended from three to five candidates to the governor. The commission evaluated each candidate by assessing integrity, maturity, job-related health issues, judicial temperament, diligence, legal knowledge, ability and experience, and community service. The governor was not required to use the commission for appellate and Supreme Court openings.

"As a commission we have visited about the [commission] procedures and how we have wanted to see the vision and the legacy," said Kathleen Meyerle, who began serving on the commission in 1991 and became chair in 1997. "I think we've all had a really strong commitment to making sure that the governor got the very best candidates that he could. One of things that motivated us was the governor's commitment to use the merit selection process."

For each appointment, Governor Carlson weighed a number of factors including scholarship, character, experience, and community involvement. But judicial activists and people who wanted to slide into retirement need not apply.

Carlson believed strongly that judges should be centrists who have the capacity to weigh a lot of arguments. He said, "I don't want people on the bench who automatically dislike business anymore than there should be anyone on the bench who dislikes certain races or certain religions or certain genders. As a society we've agreed to the latter proposition, but we haven't agreed to the former—and that bothers me. They're not up there to exercise a political agenda."

Diversity and balance became familiar terms to those involved in the selection process. Carlson appointed the first Asian-

American judge, Tony Leung, as well as many other minorities and women. Carlson also sought out attorneys with private-practice experience, as opposed to public-sector experience, in order to bring some private enterprise and management skills into the government's judicial branch.

"We never ask people about their politics," Carlson said. "We never ask where they stand on abortion, for example. But we are sensitive to other concerns. You have to be sensitive to issues of gender, race, and so forth. And, you've got to be sensitive to the needs of the bench. The goal is to plug up whatever weaknesses currently exist in the system and to provide whatever balance you possibly can."

Carlson also was sensitive to the changes in the judiciary. Today's trial court judges contend with a caseload that is very different from what their predecessors faced. "It's not an easy job," Keith said. "It takes a very skilled, patient, fair, and really a very gifted person to deal day after day after day with criminal matters, juvenile hearings, and all kinds of family problems. This is what the bulk of their work is going to be."

Selecting judges who were "of the community" also marked Carlson's tenure. "The governor was not looking for someone who had just practiced law and didn't give back to his community," noted Gilbert. "And if those judicial applicants hadn't demonstrated leadership by helping out in church, in the community, in volunteer work, in mentoring, they had very little chance of being appointed to a judgeship."

A COMMUNITY EVENT

The importance of community also played a role in the initial interview process and the final announcement. Before Carlson took office, all interviews and announcements took place in St. Paul. Carlson's commission traveled to the districts to conduct interviews.

The governor also made it standard practice to personally interview each finalist for a district court appointment. Each of the approximately 350 finalists spent about 10 minutes with the governor, lieutenant governor, and members of his staff. "The governor wanted to look each finalist in the eye and make his own personal assessment of his or her character, ability, and also humility before he would make the appointment," Gilbert said. "If an applicant came in there and told the governor he thought everything was fine with the judicial system, it might as well be a short interview, because the governor didn't think everything was fine. He was looking for some change.

"The governor was looking for thoughtful people, creative people, people who had thought about some of the problems, and who had some suggestions for change. He could tell when people were getting to the essence of a problem. And when they got to the essence of the problem, they would get the governor's attention," Gilbert said.

Once the selection process was complete, Carlson traveled to the districts to announce the appointments. In addition to underscoring the importance of the occasion, the out-state announcements drew many spectators and gave out-state media a chance to talk to the governor. "To select a judge in most of the outstate areas, it's a pretty big deal, because that person has significant standing in the community," noted Judge Terry Dempsey of the Fifth District and a former legislator. "When I was sworn in here in St. James, the courtroom was filled with people. In the middle of the week at 2:00 in the afternoon, getting 250 people from all over the county was significant."

It will be years before the full significance of Carlson's judiciary legacy becomes clear. Carlson hopes that time will demonstrate that his appointments set a standard for quality, that the people he chose have served in a thoughtful and generous way, that they have focused on the right changes for the court as well as for the public, and that they have protected both the independence and the majesty of the courts.

"The governor's legacy in the judiciary will be that he did it right," Gilbert said. "He set a course when he was first elected governor. He established his standards and he stayed on course for eight years. He appointed leaders in place. He appointed excellent lawyers in place who are going to have a major impact, not only now, but for years and years to come."

CHAPTER FOURTEEN

THE PUBLIC'S HOUSE

Carlsons Maintain Public Residence, Private Home

"**I**'m hungry," said 7-year-old Jessica Carlson as she and her parents toured the elegant Governor's Residence on Summit Avenue in January 1991. It was the first time they had seen the large Tudor-style house that is the official residence of Minnesota's governor. The family planned to move into the big house soon after the governor's swearing-in ceremony.

"There are apples downstairs in the kitchen," said Barbara Hoffmann, a lively woman who had worked for Governors Rudy Perpich and Wendell Anderson, and now helped the Carlsons get accustomed to their new roles.

For a moment, the little girl hesitated. "I'm afraid I'll get lost," she said.

Living in a public house, like the Governor's Residence, required navigation skills. Not only did the family find its way around a 12,000-square-foot mansion that was under 24-hour watch by the state patrol, but the Carlsons had to chart a course between public responsibilities and family privacy, between creating a welcoming space for all Minnesotans and living in a home of their own. In these unusual circumstances, Susan and Arne

Carlson faced the added responsibility of raising their youngest daughter as normally as possible. It was a challenge. Not every little girl could eat lunch with Arnold Schwartzenegger or have a chef scramble eggs or make pancakes for breakfast every morning.

The Carlsons were the sixth gubernatorial family to live in the mansion since the Irvine Family donated the house to the state in 1965. The house was built between 1910 and 1912 at a cost of $50,000. An example of Beaux Arts style, Minnesota architect William Channing Whitney designed the residence as his interpretation of a English Tudor country home. The residence was built with more than 20 rooms on its four finished levels, 10 bathrooms, a carriage house, and a large yard and garden.

During the Carlson administration, the house functioned as an extension of the governor's office as well as his official residence for entertaining. Governor Carlson often conducted staff meetings or budget discussions over breakfast or lunch at the residence. He also used the residence as a site for crucial meetings about state issues.

For instance, negotiations to help keep Northwest Airlines in Minnesota occurred at the residence. When bus drivers from the Metropolitan Transit Commission went on strike in 1993, Governor Carlson brought management and labor together at the residence to work out an agreement to end the strike. They met there for most of a day, before Governor Carlson came in at 10:00 P.M. to help complete the negotiations.

"It was very intentional to bring the talks to the residence," said Hoffmann, who ran the residence with its staff of eight for the Carlsons from 1992 to 1998. "It's a very safe place, and a special place." The residence was used in a similar way in July 1998 when the Minnesota State College and University system faced a possible strike by faculty.

The Carlsons instituted several rules to keep the residence a safe and special place. The Carlsons greeted every guest at the front door. Evening events were always social with spouses of guests included.

The residence was also Governor Carlson's favorite place to

honor Minnesotans. Some are well known in sports, business, or entertainment. Earl Olson, the founder of Jennie-O Foods, was an honoree as was David Wheaton, Minnesota's gift to the tennis world. University of Minnesota sports teams were treated to receptions and lunches by their number-one fan. Foreign dignitaries also have visited the residence, including former British Prime Minister Margaret Thatcher.

Most of the guests at the residence were ordinary Minnesotans. Because Susan Carlson's work focused on children and Governor Carlson loved having children around, many events at the residence involved young guests. Governor and Susan Carlson frequently challenged classes of children to do extra reading. If they completed their assignments, the students earned lunch with the governor at the residence. One of the most touching events was when children waiting to be adopted, known as Minnesota's Waiting Children, visited the residence for a holiday party. At least for an evening, they were treated to an opportunity not many others had. Also during different holidays, the Carlsons exchanged visits with St. Joseph's Home for Children, a foster care facility in Minneapolis.

On one visit, the governor stood out on the front steps of the residence, waving the children in.

"His focus is completely on the children," said Joan Jendro, who accompanied the children that day. "For the kids, the visit changed from the awe of seeing this huge mansion to this very friendly man saying, 'C'mon, c'mon, we're waiting for you.' They felt so welcomed and so comfortable."

The visits always included a beautiful banquet of children's food served on nice china and milk served in glass goblets. At Christmas, Carlson invited Gopher Basketball Coach Clem Haskins and a couple of players to meet the kids. They signed autographs and danced with the children during the afternoon. When the children presented Carlson with a thank- you card they had each signed, he read each child's name out loud. "There are a lot of kids here who consider him a friend," Jendro said.

A highlight of holiday events was always the appearance of Santa Claus or the Easter Bunny—also known as Trooper Paul Blasing, who served in the Governor's Executive Protection Detail. In addition to meeting with groups, the Carlsons opened the residence to the public several times each year. Their Halloween Open House quickly grew into a crowded event that attracted people from all over the state. For Halloween, the residence staff put on their spookiest costumes and decorated the house with cobwebs and goblins. In some years, as many as 10,000 trick-or-treaters walked through the residence to collect a bag of treats from Governor Carlson. Hoffmann estimated that 150,000 Minnesotans visited the residence during the Carlson administration.

With so many events and guests, the residence endured much wear-and-tear. Throughout the years, the residence needed repairs and redecoration. The Governor's Residence Council oversaw all changes during the Carlson years. The Carlsons along with the 1006 Summit Avenue Society, a nonprofit group to benefit the residence, raised money for the projects. One of the major fund-raisers was Susan Carlson's cookbook, *Minnesota Times and Tastes*. During the Carlson years, many projects were completed. One of the largest projects was restoring the oak paneling in the foyer to its original color, creating a warm and inviting place to greet guests. The first-floor library was redone with comfortable leather furniture, making it the ideal place for small groups to meet and talk. New dining room chairs and drapes and crystal chandeliers were added. Due to Susan Carlson's interest in the history of the residence, the lower level houses display cases and collages containing memorabilia and photographs from previous administrations, as well as honoring the state's first ladies by hanging their portraits on the wall.

One of the Carlsons' favorite additions to the residence was the Children's Garden. Dedicated in 1993, the garden featured stepping stones, small wood and iron sculptures of children, a pond, and banks of cutting flowers. A pathway lined with boulders led visitors through the garden, paying tribute to the families who have called 1006 Summit Avenue home. Many of the plants were chosen because they would seem fun to children, such as balloon flowers and plants that encourage butterflies to settle in the garden. The garden was a tangible statement of the

Carlsons commitment to children in the state, and it was the place in the sprawling back yard Governor Carlson was most likely to show off to guests.

During the governor's first term, the residence was the Carlsons' only home, although they kept a cabin in Wisconsin for occasional retreats. Jessica was only 7 when the Carlsons moved in, and the residence staff enjoyed having a child around. Cabbage Patch dolls once flanked the fence surrounding the house and troll dolls peaked out of Jessica's bedroom window. On the first warm day of spring one year, Jessica and her friends romped in the garden fountain until a groundskeeper told the girls they would be electrocuted if they played there. (Not true, but it got them out of the fountain.) Because the Carlsons wanted Jessica to live like a normal child, with normal responsibilities and expectations, her parents asked her to pick up her own room and always clear her own dishes.

The staff of the residence quickly became like family to the Carlsons. Each morning the governor bantered with the two chefs who prepared meals at the residence. He frequently spent a few moments sipping coffee in the small breakfast nook in the kitchen. Carlson's adult children, Anne and Tucker, also had fond memories of the residence. Both lived in the house for short periods during the governor's tenure in office. In addition, Anne held her wedding reception at the residence after her marriage to Andrew Davis in 1993. In 1997, the family celebrated Tucker's marriage to Monica Duvall in the garden of the residence.

For Carlson, three events demonstrated the atmosphere of welcome that he and Susan strived to achieve at the residence.

The first was the annual visit of the Gopher football team. Held early in the season, the University of Minnesota Band played the "Minnesota Rouser" as the players entered the residence, and Susan and Governor Carlson greeted them at the door. Carlson always invited former Gophers who delivered pep talks to the players. Minnesota Coach Glen Mason once remarked that in 25 years of coaching, he had never been invited to a governor's residence, much less with an entire team.

The other two events took place during the busy fall of 1996. On

September 13, Governor and Susan Carlson hosted an elegant luncheon for King Carl XVI Gustaf and Queen Silvia of Sweden. The Swedish monarchs came to Minnesota to help dedicate a park in Chisago City in honor of the writer Vilhelm Moberg, who wrote several novels about Swedish immigrants. The event showcased Minnesota both through the menu and entertainment.

During all the preparations for the visit, the emissaries of King Carl Gustaf and Queen Silvia made it clear that the king never spoke at these kinds of events. However, at the end of the luncheon, the King asked Susan Carlson if it would be acceptable for him to say a few words. He thanked the Carlsons and their guests for one of the most enjoyable visits he had ever had in America. "Because we knew that was something he never did, it was a very special event," Carlson said. The Carlsons developed such a rapport with the monarchs that the King and Queen invited the governor and Susan to their palace in Stockholm.

Two weeks later, the Carlsons hosted a more solemn and moving event. After watching the movie *Schindler's List*, the governor and daughter Jessica, who was then in junior high school, talked about the holocaust. She wondered if any Minnesotans were holocaust survivors. "Of course," the governor said, and that exchange sparked the idea of holding a reception to honor Minnesota's holocaust survivors. It was the first time any state had officially honored those who survived the holocaust. Working with local Jewish groups, the Governor extended an invitation to all holocaust survivors living in Minnesota. The evening's program included several survivors sharing their stories. Carlson noted how all the survivors mentioned the element of luck in living through the ordeal.

"We are the lucky ones," Carlson said at the time. "We are lucky they are here to tell us their stories so we can ensure that this tragedy never happens again."

After eight years of living at the residence, the Carlsons have many fond memories. Whether they were greeting foreign heads of state, dancing and singing with visiting children, or honoring community leaders, each event added to the history of Minnesota's house.

CHAPTER FIFTEEN

THE NUMBER ONE FAN

Carlson Goes to Bat for Sports and the Arts in Minnesota

As newly elected Governor Arne Carlson and his wife, Susan, walked into the Minneapolis Convention Center to celebrate his inauguration on January 12, 1991, the University of Minnesota Marching Band struck up the "Minnesota Rouser," the University of Minnesota fight song. Thus, at the earliest possible moment of his administration, the governor served notice that he would be completely partisan when it came to the Minnesota Gophers. As if to underscore the point, one of the first parties the Carlsons held in their new residence on Summit Avenue was for the University of Minnesota men's basketball team.

Throughout his eight years as governor, political winds shifted and alliances came and went, but one thing, one loyalty, remained intact and unshakable: The Governor was the Gopher's First Fan.

"When I think about the last eight years," said McKinley Boston, vice president for student development and athletics at the University of Minnesota, "I really can't think of anyone who helped us move the agenda forward more than Governor Carlson has. He understood the value of athletics to the quality of life in a community."

"We go way back," said University Basketball Coach Clem Haskins. "He's my friend. When we go to lunch, we talk about basketball, but we talk about other things too. Once in a lifetime you get a governor like him."

That the Gophers—particularly the basketball Gophers—held a special place in Carlson's heart is obvious to anyone who paid the least attention to University athletics. Gopher basketball games invariably showed up as must-do events on his schedule every winter, and Minnesotans often saw their governor loudly cheering the team from his seat at side court, a few rows behind the Gopher bench. (Carlson's love for the team extended to its venue, Williams Arena. "There's no other place like it for watching a basketball game," he said. "In the Barn, fans really can be the sixth player.") If the team went on to play in a postseason tournament, the governor was sure to be among the fans attend-

A COMMUNITY FOR THE ARTS

Quality of life is measured in more than wins and losses, however. Despite dealing with an enormous budget shortfall during his first term, Carlson displayed a support, albeit a restrained support, for the arts.

"He didn't single out the arts board for pain," said Conrad (Connie) Razidlo, a retired advertising executive and member of the Minnesota State Arts Board at that time. "We went through those tough times with everybody else. Then, in 1993, the legislature voted to increase the arts budget by 55 percent. Arne could have vetoed that, but he passively acquiesced. I've known Arne for a lifetime, and he's not particularly interested in the arts. He's not a highbrow and he never pretended that he was."

But Carlson recognized that the arts, like sports, can help unify a community. With encouragement from Razidlo and others, he allowed the Governor's Residence on St. Paul's Summit Avenue to become a Minnesota art gallery. Works of state artists were frequently displayed in the public rooms of the residence. He also hosted opening night events for artists and performers.

ing some or all of the games, no matter where they were played. He wore his maroon-and-gold letter sweater in the office nearly everyday. He wrote letters to criticize officiating at games and sometimes made his opinion on athletic department issues known in public.

Carlson and his wife, Susan, supported women's athletics as well, including attending the dedication of the Women's Sports Pavilion and the annual Berg Banquet. Susan, a standout athlete in high school and college, traveled with the Gopher women's basketball team when it went to its first National Collegiate Athletic Association game at Notre Dame.

"Every governor can and will find a way to support the most bonding elements of a community," said Women's Athletic Director Chris Voelz. "Each will find a way, though [he or she] might have different favorite sports. Some governors will be oriented more toward policy than personal presence; others, more toward presence than policy. I think Governor Carlson will be distinctive in his zeal."

Carlson's ongoing support for university athletics was person-

Carlson also knew that the arts had a significant economic impact. He recognized the economic value, for instance, of the film industry. Feature film production had pumped more than $36 million into Minnesota's economy between 1994 and 1996. So Carlson went to Hollywood, where he met with officials from Universal, New Line, Paramount, and Warner, cheerleading his state's attributes. The state had continued to be a significant site for filming, with productions like *Grumpy Old Men*, its sequel *Grumpier Old Men*, and Arnold Schwartzenegger's *Jingle All the Way* using the state for location shots.

Sometimes, the governor even mingled with the stars. During the filming of *Grumpier Old Men*, Carlson met Ann Margaret. Normally reserved and unwilling to do impromptu events, Ann Margaret was thrilled to meet a governor who shared her Swedish ancestry. When she heard Carlson had arrived, she burst from her dressing room at the sound stage at Paisley Park, greeted the surprised governor with a kiss, and

al and sometimes "fatherly," said University President Mark Yudof, who sat next to the governor when the men's basketball Gophers lost to the University of Kentucky in the NCAA semifinals in 1997. "He's one hundred and ten percent maroon and gold," Yudof said. "The governor genuinely admires athletes, men or women, and he admires student athletes who can make it through [the University]. When you puff up a little about winning the NIT or whatever, you puff up about the whole mission of the university. Obviously, you need a balance. You don't want to put all your eggs in one basket and starve the English department. But I never doubted where his loyalties lay, and that is to making this place as good as it can be."

The First Fan believed that sports, like other community activities, could unify a state. He included professional sports in that assessment, though with some qualification. "Pro sports are largely economic," Carlson said. "My interest in them is more as a governor, in that I perceive they're important on two levels. The first is economic; the second is social—[the ability of pro sports] to draw people together, as do all sports. In order to have a com-

began an animated conversation in Swedish.

As budget worries eased in his second term, Carlson decided it was time to bring the arts to the communities. "I was listening to a program in which Tony Randall was talking about American theater and how much he would like to see communities develop the American theater," said Carlson. Randall's radio speech struck a chord with Carlson, whose father had been a lover of opera and theater. "It was always my father's belief that you should build more in the way of community theater."

In the spring of 1996, the governor called Sam Grabarski, then the executive director of the Minnesota State Arts Board, and asked him, along with Razidlo and arts activist Larry Redmond, to design a plan for bolstering Minnesota's arts community.

"He handed the reins over to us, but he wanted to make it clear he supported this" said Redmond, a lobbyist for Minnesota Citizens for the Arts, an association of all the state's nonprofit arts organizations. "He was enthusiastic, but he munity, we have to have a community of interests. We've been going through a period where our society's focus has been on individual selfishness and greed. 'What can I do for me?' I think we're beginning to understand that there is a 'we.' Sports has the potential to bring people together."

Of course, so do arts, music, theater, parks, trails, and all of the other elements that contribute to a community's quality of life. Such elements, though hard to measure, nevertheless make the state a better place to live and a more attractive place for companies to settle in and to create high-quality jobs in. When Carlson referred to Des Moines as "dead" in 1997, his intention was not to incur the wrath of Iowans (which he did), but to remind Minnesotans that our state offers an unusually rich cultural life. Carlson pursued many paths to keep Minnesota lively during his eight years in office.

KEEPING THE TIMBERWOLVES

The governor's first major pro sports challenge came in 1993, when Norm Green packed up and moved the National Hockey

was concerned with accountability. He wanted to be sure this wouldn't be an elitist program and that there would be an actual, ongoing, and meaningful contribution to the quality of life for Minnesotans."

Later that summer, the three reported back to the governor at a luncheon meeting at the residence. The plan was to add $12 million—an astonishing 89 percent increase—into the budget. "I said, 'Sounds good. Let's go with it,'" recalled Carlson. The money was used to stabilize the funding of arts organizations in the state and to create Arts Across Minnesota, a series of annual, ongoing festivals throughout the state. With backing from Arts Across Minnesota, organizations like the St. Paul Chamber Orchestra were to perform all around the state. In addition, communities were to take turns in creating their own celebrations of artistic creativity.

The governor announced the initiative in late 1996, and the Minnesota Legislature approved it in 1997. In 1996, the governor also made one more sales pitch for Minnesota. State arts groups had

League's Minnesota North Stars to Dallas after the team had played 26 years at the old Met Center in Bloomington. Determined to never again see his state lose a big-league professional sports franchise, that fall Carlson appointed Henry Savelkoul, a moderate Republican and longtime legislative ally, to the Metropolitan Sports Facilities Commission. Savelkoul, a lawyer from Albert Lea, had served six terms in the legislature during which he'd built a reputation as a person who knew how to close a deal.

Savelkoul's mission, Carlson said at the time, was to get an NHL team back in Minnesota, find a way to refinance the Target Center, and keep Minnesota's other professional teams in the state.

A few months later, in February 1994, the glitterati of the professional basketball world gathered in Minneapolis for the National Basketball Association's All-Star Weekend. Carlson took in the festivities, but his attendance wasn't just for amusement. The 5-year-old NBA home team, the Timberwolves, was

been courting Disney, which was planning a stage adaptation of its hit movie *The Lion King*, said Fred Krohn, general manager of the State and Orpheum theaters. Krohn had talked with midlevel managers at Disney but knew that Disney Chief Executive Officer Michael Eisner would make the final decision. Eisner is notoriously difficult to reach.

"I went to Governor Carlson and said, is there a way you might invite Michael Eisner to your residence," Krohn recalled. "He said he'd be glad to do that. So, on the evening of the opening of *Beauty and the Beast*, I was able to spend a half hour by the fire in the Governor's Residence with the governor and Michael Eisner. That was instrumental to our getting *The Lion King*, and the rest is history. It wouldn't have happened without the governor."

Carlson's support for the arts earned him an award from the Americans for the Arts and the U.S. Conference of Mayors in 1997. "I wanted more money to drift down to smaller communities for whatever visions they had," Carlson said of his arts initiative.

"They say that arts are the soul of a community," Carlson said when he received the award, "and it's true." ■

struggling both on the court and in the business ledgers. The co-owners, Marv Wolfenson and Harvey Ratner, had said they couldn't keep up with the debt payments on the Timberwolves' $104 million home in downtown Minneapolis, the Target Center. Wolfenson and Ratner had talked about selling the Timberwolves to potential buyers who planned to move the team to New Orleans. The sale would go through unless the City of Minneapolis took over the building. During the All-Star Game, as the governor and First Lady Susan Carlson sat in center-court seats, the governor strategized with NBA Commissioner David Stern. They agreed that they both wanted the Timberwolves to stay in Minnesota. But how could they make that happen?

The governor asked Savelkoul, Minneapolis businessman Bob Dayton, and John Moir, financial officer for Minneapolis, to come up with a financing plan that the city, the state, and the Metropolitan Sports Facilities Commission all could support. The 18,000-seat arena meant jobs and revenue for Minneapolis. It had significantly revitalized a dead area of downtown. Keeping it solvent was important for the state, not just the city, Carlson thought.

For nearly a year after Ratner and Wolfenson put the team on the market, plans were floated and shot down. The most promising had been a plan negotiated by Twin Cities businessmen Bill Sexton and Willis Heim. That deal stalled, however, when the prospective buyers in New Orleans threatened legal action. Then, in early August 1994, Mankato businessman and former state legislator Glen Taylor swept into the picture. In a slam-dunk deal, he agreed to virtually the same arrangement Sexton had asked for, and Ratner and Wolfenson agreed.

In about a week's time, Taylor made a deal to buy the Timberwolves for $88 million, and the Metropolitan Sports Facilities Commission agreed to buy the Target Center for $54 million. As a part of the agreement, Taylor promised that the Wolves wouldn't leave the state for a period of at least 30 years, unless during that time property taxes increased by more than 2 percent a year over a 5-year period.

"The governor's involvement was greater before I entered the picture," Taylor said. "He really wanted to show that Minnesota was the place [for the Timberwolves to be]. He went to the NBA Board of Governors and persuaded them that the state of Minnesota would [participate in efforts to keep them here]. He personally went to New York and bought some extra time so that a deal could be put together. When he heard my name mentioned, he called me and asked, 'What can I do?' I told him, 'I don't think you have to do anything.' I give him credit. He made sure the team stayed here."

"I think he's been very good for Minnesota sports," said Taylor. When people tried to downplay the importance of pro sports, or to insist that there were other, and higher, priorities to attend to, "the governor said, 'No, this is a part of our culture and a part of our economy.'" Carlson fought hard to keep the team here, even though "that was not necessarily the popular thing to do," Taylor noted.

Having successfully kept the Timberwolves in the state, Carlson was on a roll in 1995. Then came the ill-fated courtship between Minnesota businessman Richard Burke and the Winnipeg Jets of the NHL. When Richard Burke and his partner, Steve Gluckstern, agreed to buy the Jets for $68 million, they knew they wanted the team to play somewhere other than in Winnipeg. Along with Minneapolis, Burke and Gluckstern considered Portland, Nashville, Atlanta, and Phoenix.

At first, Carlson suggested that the state give back to the team about $1.8 million a year from income taxes, up to as much as $15 million. Although legislators had qualms about the plan, many thought that it would make the deal sweet enough to attract a team.

It didn't. In the fall of 1995, Burke asked for $8 million a year. That sum far outweighed the amount of public money going to the Timberwolves, and meant, in effect, that the public would be buying the team about every eight years. Morrie Anderson, then the governor's chief of staff, called attention to the difference between what he called an "eternal subsidy" and the public investment in Target Center or a new stadium for the Twins. The obvious lack of support sent Burke looking elsewhere. He and the Jets eventually landed in Phoenix, where the team was reborn as the Coyotes.

STADIUM AT BAT

The Twins and their supporters, some of whom were in the state legislature, began pushing in 1995 for a referendum on a new stadium. Twins owner, Carl Pohlad, said the team couldn't make money in the Metrodome because too much of the revenue from the stadium went to the Metropolitan Sports Facilities Commission and the Vikings. The Twins played in the dome rent-free, but they got no money from parking or luxury suites. Only a portion of stadium advertising revenues went to the Twins and they paid a 10 percent tax on ticket revenues. The Twins had been losing about $10 million a year at the Metrodome and would continue to do so as long as they had to play in that building, Pohlad said. He began talking about selling the Twins once they were free of the Metrodome lease in 1998.

Carlson and a bipartisan group of legislators agreed to push for a referendum as a way to keep the Twins at home. Representative Ann Rest, DFL-New Hope, was the chief author in the House of a bill that called for a nonbinding referendum in the seven-county metro area to test public support for building a stadium. By March 1996, the referendum proposal was defeated in a House committee and support for it was waning in the Senate.

So, the governor changed course. He encouraged legislators to come up with a proposal that the legislature could vote on in 1997.

"The governor was a strong advocate for a stadium," said House Speaker Phil Carruthers, DFL-Brooklyn Center, "and that took a lot of guts—to come out so strongly in favor of it."

Said Senate Majority Leader Roger Moe of Erskine, "He didn't want the Twins to leave on his watch. Like me, he views them as an asset to the state and the region. They financially aren't going to make it without a new stadium and they're worth saving, although not at any cost."

Rest, like the governor, believed that baseball was the last professional sport to be priced low enough for average families to enjoy. "Baseball more than any other team sport is oriented toward family affordability," Rest said. "That makes it unique among professional sports." It also made it worth going to bat for the Twins.

With legislative leaders and Carlson behind the idea, plans

began forming. A retractable roof was an early component, along with a mix of public and private funding. With a price tag of about $350 million, the administration estimated it could be paid for in seven or eight years.

In his 1997 State of the State address, Carlson laid out the specifics. He wanted a 10-cent tax on cigarettes to buy 49 percent of the Twins and a $350 million dollar stadium for them to play in. The issue dominated talk-radio shows and legislative discussions during the winter of 1997. But in the end, both the House and Senate tax committees voted down plans for funding a new Twins stadium.

Ideas that would have used proceeds from slot machines at Canterbury Park, a Twin Cities horse-racing track and casino, and even the governor's favorite, the tax on cigarettes, all were turned down, some vigorously. It didn't help that the estimated cost of a new stadium had now risen to about $439 million for a facility with a retractable roof because of new construction estimates and revised interest rate forecasts. Opponents of the stadium portrayed any public assistance at all as "corporate welfare" for a billionaire.

"The pressures against any kind of public participation were overwhelming," said Rest. "There were very many and varied interests opposing the stadium, and the pro-stadium strategy was not always focused. The Twins deal was a part of the legislative process and, you name it, everybody had an oar in there. I think it just crumbled under its own weight."

In September, Pohlad signed a letter of intent with North Carolina businessman Don Beaver. Although Pohlad insisted that he didn't want the Twins to move, the agreement with Beaver called for the North Carolinian to take the team home with him if the legislature didn't approve a stadium deal by November 30, 1997. This set the stage for a special legislative session specifically to consider the stadium issue.

STADIUM STRIKES OUT

In October, Pohlad threw another curve ball that quickly enlivened the discussion. While proposing to a joint House-

Senate committee that the Twins contribute $111 million toward a $411 million retractable-roof stadium, Pohlad mentioned that he would consider giving the team to the state or to a nonprofit organization—if the state would take on the $80 million of debt the team had accumulated.

Carlson quickly seconded the idea, and bipartisan support sprang up from Senate Majority Leader Moe and House Speaker Carruthers. But the optimism was shortlived. During a special session in October, legislators voted down every proposal to fund a stadium. They even voted down a bill that would have sent the issue to the voters, via a referendum.

Carruthers flatly told newspaper reporters, "There won't be public financing of a new stadium." The Vikings, meanwhile, had stirred up more public discussion by hinting that they would need a new facility soon too.

After the legislature recessed for two weeks, the Twins continued talks with Beaver while also pleading with Minnesotans through an advertising campaign. When the second special session reconvened in November 1997, however, the answer was the same: "No" to any plan for any public support of a Twins' stadium. "No" from Republicans and "No" from DFLers. The "No" was bipartisan and overwhelming, but the scant support was bipartisan too.

"It was an excellent package," Carlson said. "It would have been a massive change for Minneapolis—all of it positive. I would do it tomorrow if I could. I don't think the issue ever was tested on the merits of the deal. It instantly got sidetracked on whether or not you liked Carl Pohlad. And whether or not you liked pro sports."

Although the governor didn't mention the Twins' stadium in his last State of the State address, no one believed the issue wouldn't arise during the 1998 legislative session. It did—briefly. Representative Loren Jennings, a DFLer from Harris who had labored for the Twins' bill during the 1997 sessions, withdrew his plan for a $234 million ballpark before a House committee could hear it when it became obvious he didn't have any support.

"I asked him [Carlson] at least 27 times to run for a third term," said Jennings. "I wish he had said 'yes.' I have nothing but the highest regard for the governor. It was fun and interesting to work with him [on the stadium issue]. He always seemed to be able to get to the heart of the issue. I probably saw him invest more of himself in this because I think he felt like baseball is important as a part of the overall fabric of society. He was concerned that if we let the naysayers tear down baseball, what will this same group of people try to tear down next week? Governor Carlson always tried to do the right thing, and that's the difference between politicians and a statesperson."

While Carlson determined that he would not get out front on the stadium issue in 1998, he remained supportive. Behind the scenes, Carlson and his top aide Bernie Omann worked with the Twins and the Metropolitan Sports Facilities Commission to find a way to keep the Twins in Minnesota—even temporarily. Omann had been the governor's representative throughout the long and frustrating negotiations for a new stadium. In July 1998, Omann, Henry Savelkoul, and Bill Lester of the sports facilities commission, reached a "consensus agreement" with the Twins. The agreement gave the Twins a two-year lease in the Metrodome and required Twins' owners to consider offers to buy the team from potential local owners for at least 30 days. While the agreement did not settle the stadium issue completely, it did give the state time to work out an arrangement that would keep the Twins in Minnesota for the long term.

Said Carlson, "There's no reason this can't work out. There really isn't."

A WIN FOR HOCKEY

The resounding defeat of any public support for a Twins stadium triggered anxiety among supporters of a proposal to build a hockey arena in St. Paul. The National Hockey League had been planning to expand the number of teams for some time. In June 1997, NHL Commissioner Gary Bettman announced that Minnesota would be one of the sites. The new team, owned by billboard magnate Bob Naegele Jr. would be in St. Paul. Naegele and St. Paul Mayor Norm Coleman had put together a plan to renovate the St. Paul Civic Center into a $130 million arena in the city's RiverCentre complex. An important element in the deal was a $65 million contribution from the state, which Carlson had agreed to deliver.

But hockey supporters began to wonder whether the "No" to the Twins stadium would ripple out and destroy the chances of getting a hockey arena in St. Paul for the newly named Minnesota Wild.

"I just basically said that if we weren't going to use general tax money for baseball, we weren't going to use it for hockey," said Moe, who opposed the deal.

Carlson countered that those opposing the hockey arena were more concerned with the political aspirations of Coleman than the merits of the deal. Coleman had recently shifted allegiances from the DFL to the Independent Republican Party and was running hard to become Carlson's successor in the governor's office. Bringing home a hockey arena surely would make Coleman look good to voters.

So Carlson held firm to his commitment to the arena and got out his favorite tool—the veto pen. He told legislators that he would veto the capital investments bonding bill if it didn't include his priorities, including the $65 million for St. Paul's RiverCentre project. The bonding bill, which is passed only every other year, included significant projects for St. Cloud, Minneapolis, and many other areas of the state—projects also on the governor's priority list. Legislators knew that Carlson—who had vetoed the vital elementary and secondary education bill in 1997—would not hesitate to veto this as well. They approved the no-interest loan from the state for the hockey arena in 1998. Carlson attributed that victory to timing and the peculiar nature of sports fans.

"Hockey fans are the most enthusiastic, passionate, uncompromising sports addicts there are," Carlson said. "They will stick with you through thick and thin. They are hard core. Baseball fans are little softer. "

"The governor stayed with us under great pressure," said Mayor Coleman. "He stood by his word under great pressure, but he had the St. Paul House delegation and the City Council behind him. The key defining moment was when the governor met with Senator Moe and Speaker Carruthers. They thought he would abandon St. Paul and they would be happy. He didn't want to veto the bonding bill, but he told them he was prepared to take drastic measures."

In the agreement, the state gave St. Paul a $65-million, interest-free loan and agreed to forgive $17 million of that as long as the arena hosts public events each year. St. Paul put up $65 million in bonds, and the team agreed to pay building costs for the arena and $6 million a year in rent and taxes.

Said Representative Loren Jennings, "St. Paul was wise enough to package the arena as a convention center that just happened to have a pro sports team in it. I think we should have packaged the stadium with the hockey arena and the convention center, but we were reacting to the Pohlads' deadlines. You can't take something so controversial and stand it out there by itself."

Jennings' DFL House colleague Rest agreed with his assessment. "The decision was made to keep the Twins stadium separate—there was no connection between the Twins stadium and anything else," said Rest. "I don't fault the governor for the process that he used or for trying to bring many interests together. I don't know that any governor could have done a better job. He was very cordial to us, very sympathetic to the travails we were going through, and he was always available."

Larry Redmond, who also worked as a lobbyist for the Twins effort, said the governor's support for the Twins stadium was not unlike his support for the arts.

"If one steps back," said Redmond, "what one sees in Arne Carlson is an attempt to try to have a well-balanced community. These are the activities that are very important to people's lives. The question is, does the state have a legislative role in making sure that they're there?"

Carlson said it does.

LEADERSHIP LESSONS

Epilogue

Arne Carlson tells a story about his days playing football for the Choate School. The team included a talented running back, but the coach benched him. The team wondered why. "He runs in a guarded way," the coach said. "He's always trying to protect himself. He'll lose the ball or injure himself running like that."

Arne Carlson never forgot that lesson. "You've got to be free enough to run with reckless abandon," Carlson said. "Take the ball and slug it over the line." For more than 30 years in public life, Arne Carlson slugged it over the line. He didn't make every touchdown he sought, and some he made by just inches. He tackled a few people along the way. Still Carlson's style of leadership—straightforward, blunt, tenacious—brought him more success than most expected when he was first elected in 1990—and more respect. "I don't always like Arne," said one Republican state senator. "But I admire what he's done and I sure am glad when he's on my side."

In his eight years as governor, Carlson developed a unique leadership style. It is not a style everyone could—or would want to—emulate. If you listen to Carlson and those around him long enough, the hallmarks of Carlson's leadership emerge.

KNOW WHAT YOU BELIEVE. Across eight years, from times of desperate economic trouble to incredible economic success, Arne Carlson gave similar State of the State addresses. Each year he talked about the same themes and initiatives. When he failed, it was because he strayed from these core beliefs. Cyndy Brucato, his press secretary for five years, remembered how in the 1993 legislative session his agenda crystalized around fiscal issues and pragmatic social policy. It worked, she said, because it was who he was. Carlson knew what he believed and he stuck to it. He did not get distracted by other issues. Since 1991, he preached the gospel of fiscal restraint. He promoted innovation in education continuously. His support for preventive programs aimed at children was as loyal as his love of the Golden Gopher basketball team. When those who served with him criticized the governor, it was usually for what he did not do. He should have moved the Republican Party to the center more. He should have completely reorganized state government, and reduced its size. He should have paid more attention to energy issues or the environment or agriculture or whatever. Maybe so. But to do those other things would have pulled Carlson's energies from his real passions—and that, he believed, would have been a mistake.

FIND PEOPLE YOU TRUST AND LET THEM GO. Arne Carlson has great leadership skills, but he does not try to micromanage issues. His personal staffers and people who worked in state agencies for him knew not to barrage the governor with details. He got bored and impatient with them. Carlson often complained about legislators who focused on the details and forgot the big picture. But details needed to be addressed, so Carlson hired people he trusted to take care of them. Bernie Omann worked with Carlson as a legislator, agency official, deputy chief of staff, and ultimately Carlson's chief of staff. Omann also helped Carlson organize his 1994 election, and admired the governor's ability to let go of the details of such a personally important job as his reelection campaign. "He knows what it takes to empower people," Omann said. "When [campaign manager] Joe Weber came in, he gave him the keys and said, 'Go do it.'"

Because Carlson willingly turned over the keys, he often called on people whom he had worked with before successfully. Consider Linda Kohl. A former newspaper reporter, she started out as director of the Minnesota Planning Agency for Carlson. She later helped with the merger of the Department of Children, Families, and Learning, then worked as Carlson's press secretary when Cyndy Brucato moved to his campaign staff for a few months. During his second term, she was involved in the merger of the Minnesota State College and University system (MnSCU) where she finally served as vice chancellor. She was one of many examples of people the governor tapped repeatedly for important assignments.

NEVER MAKE THE SAME MISTAKE TWICE. When Carlson had 14 vetoes ruled illegal because a deadline had been missed, he took a vow: That will never happen again. By 1992, his staff had in place an elaborate system to track bills and vetoes to ensure that every bill was handled properly. It was the most often noted example of a characteristic many people said the governor possesses. He did not make the same mistake twice. From his failures and missteps, Carlson learned new, better ways to operate. In 1991 and into 1992, Carlson often felt he was out-front and alone on key issues, like fiscal restraint, workers' compensation reform, and school innovation. So he hired a staff person to help him build coalitions of groups and individuals who cared about the same issues he did. Those coalitions not only supported his proposals as they moved through the legislature, but they became sources of ideas and information that he used to improve proposals.

USE THE TOOLS YOU HAVE. Carlson always wondered why other governors failed to use the veto as a tool to get legislative approval of their programs. Carlson used the veto a record 179 times without being overridden. He used the threat of the veto enough to get cooperation from the legislature. "They didn't put that veto in the Constitution so we could admire it," he said. "It was there to be used." As governor, he used the bully pulpit, the appointment process, and the majesty of the office to get what he wanted done. He often said that one governor should be able to run a lot faster than 201 legislators, and Carlson relied on the tools of office to do that.

DON'T LET OTHERS DICTATE YOUR STYLE. "Dr. No." "Governor Grumpy." "Smart and mean." Arne Carlson's personal style was the source of plenty of political humor and some mean-spiritedness during his eight years as governor. He doesn't care and he's not going to change. If you worry too much about what others think of you, you spend your life re-making yourself, Carlson said. "And what have you accomplished then?" Besides, your faults can be a strength. "I'm blunt. I'm bottom line–oriented. I'm impatient. Sometimes that saves a lot of time," Carlson said. "People know if they come to see me we're not going to chitchat for 20 minutes. They get right to it."

COMPLETE THE CIRCLE. Carlson believed that life is circular, that we come around to the point where we started, and that how we make that connection is important to our own sense of accomplishment and worth.

When Arne Carlson proposed boarding schools to put at-risk youth in a disciplined, academically focused environment, he must have been thinking about a young boy from the Bronx who was pulled from an unhappy, poverty-stricken home and given a chance to learn in a stable school environment. His work on school choice, he said, was directly related to his own experience. The camp counselors at St. Andrew's Camp and the teachers at the Choate School saved him from being one of society's throwaway children. To close the circle, Carlson wanted to do the same for poor children in Minnesota. School choice, he said, "is the civil rights issue of the 1990s." He was willing to go anywhere and talk to any group to promote school choice. That's how he was closing that circle.

LET GO WHEN IT'S TIME. Each generation has its moment and each has its time to move on. Politicians, more than others, tend to linger too long, Carlson said. Scores of people asked Arne Carlson to run for a third term in office. The temptation was there. He would miss the thrill of the battle and the stimulation and satisfaction that come from making a difference in policy. He would miss facing off against legislators and pulling out his veto pen. He would even miss dueling with the media. He resisted temptation because he felt the risk in staying past his time was too great. "After you've been there a while, it would be easy to get lazy or to not take as much care as you should, or the people around you might get careless and something could happen," Carlson said. He wanted to leave office feeling proud of what had been accomplished—not for himself. Letting go after two terms was for his three children—Tucker, Anne, and Jessica.

"The way things are now, I think they can go through life feeling good about the Carlson name," he said. "Think about the Nixon daughters and what a burden that name was for them."

Arne Carlson wanted his name to be a source of joy for all his children, and so he let go.

A CONVERSATION WITH GOVERNOR CARLSON

Carlson Speaks Out about His Eight Years in Office

In late July 1998, Governor Carlson talked with editor Mary Lahr Schier about his administration and his thoughts on leaving public office. Here is a transcript of the conversation.

Q: In one of our earliest conversations, you mentioned that you always wanted to be governor during a time of transition. Why? And have the last eight years been a transitional period?

A: A transition is a period of time when there is an intense, pressured change and virtually all institutions, not just political institutions, come out of the transition changed. The most radical transitions in my lifetime were, in a political sense, the New Deal and then the aftermath of World War II. So if you could look at America in 1927 and again in 1947, you wouldn't recognize it.

We obviously have not gone through that large a transition in the last 8, 10, or 12 years. But what we have done is made substantive changes in how we do business. For whatever reason, and I can't put my finger on it, 1990 was kind of a watershed year. During the 1980s, all over America most states were spending more than they were taking in. In 1990, a whole group of new governors came in and many, many of those states had a financial crisis. Minnesota wasn't the worst, but we certainly had a crisis with a $1.8 billion deficit. And I think a lot of governors concluded that devolution—a transfer of power from the federal government to the states had to take place. You had governors, like Tommy Thompson in Wisconsin, who had experimented in the area of welfare, and a lot of governors on both sides of the aisle were captivated by that possibility. I was very much impressed at the first National Governor's Association meeting where the focus was on health care. I began to realize that the way to handle the budget crisis was to get at the cost drivers in the system. In order to get budget stability, we had to have a series of reforms. Ultimately, that drive for budget stability was what got us into health care reform, welfare reform, workers' compensation reform, and eventually education. As it turned out, we accomplished more statewide reforms in this state than any other.

Q: Health care reform was really your first big reform effort. Why did you take that on?

A: My personal goal in 1992 was not to do health care. I wanted just a small experiment. But then the legislature crammed that dreadful bill through in 1991 that would have cost us $500 million for basically a single- payer system and we didn't have a revenue source. So, I asked [then Health Commissioner] Marlene Marschall to put together a group to redesign our bill. She did a magnificent job. She was one of the real heroines of the early years. She was very grandmotherly and knew the system top to bottom. Everybody trusted her. I think once everybody saw her report, they got serious and decided, "gee, maybe we can do this."

Q: What do you see as your most important accomplishments as governor?

A: Emotionally, the top one has to be education. As I have told you before, I see life as a circle. The older I get, the more I realize that I'm trying to close the circle—going back to my days as a kid, the places we lived, my years at the Choate School and what a tremendous difference that made in my life. Just think of the possibilities of being able to offer all children the same kind of opportunity I had. To me, that was the most rewarding moment.

The second thing would be the financial piece—that we have taken the state from a $1.8 billion deficit to a $2.3 billion surplus in 1997, $1.9 billion surplus in 1998. Now my critics would say I was helped along by a good economy, and I was. But the difference is that early on we identified indices that would limit the growth of state spending. Remember, we vetoed over $1.5 billion in spending, which, by the way, would have had a compound effect. We'd still be talking deficits without that. We wouldn't have that AAA bond rating back. That was an outside verification that "Yes, you've done a good job managing your financial resources."

Q: On finances, several people have told me that you have changed the culture of "tax and spend" at the Capitol. Do you think you have?

A: I would say that is a very accurate observation. The dynamic that used to take place at the Capitol was that everything was defined in the context of the needs of providers. All the various groups would petition state government for this, this, and that. By and large, the media is sympathetic to these requests. "Oh, we need more money for education." Well, who is against that? "Oh, we need more money for the poor." Fine, I'm for that. There was virtually no focus on the outcomes. We tried to do two things. First, we said we are not going to spend more money than we have. Second, we put the focus on the outcomes. What is it that we get for this? For example, the whole welfare debate put the focus on outcomes. That dynamic has changed forever.

Q: Do you think the state will go back to the old way of doing business after you've left office?

A: I don't think so. We have made some fundamental changes and I don't see any willingness to go back. That isn't to say there aren't people in the provider system who wouldn't love to turn the clock back. They would.

Q: Some of the DFL candidates for governor have talked about rolling back your education reforms, specifically the tax credits and deductions. Do you have any fear about the future of those programs?

A: That's just pandering to the teachers' unions, and yes, it's very threatening. But once you have started the idea of doing standardized testing and getting parents involved, they become a powerful part of the equation. I think it would be very difficult for any governor to come to the legislature and say, "I'm going to take away these tax benefits. We're not going to help parents pay for a tutor for their child anymore. We're not going to help them buy a computer. We're not going to help them pay for private education." Bear in mind, many of those candidates were the benefactors of private education. At some point, the respected media will raise questions about the hypocrisy.

Q: You recently started a promotional campaign to make parents more familiar with the tax credits and deductions. Was that to prevent a rollback in the future?

A: It's a very powerful tool. Parents will find out about it. My wife was looking at a new computer recently and the clerk in the store reminded her she could deduct the cost of it using the education deduction. So, it's happening. The word is getting out. You've got to get parents involved. You can't just plow money into the schools and say it's all theirs. We did that for 50, 60 years and we did not like the outcomes. I think we have one of the most exciting plans in America right now.

Q: Will you continue your work for school choice after you leave office?

A: Yes, I'll be a member of the board of directors of the National School Choice Foundation, which is a volunteer position. I intend to travel and speak out on school choice as much as time permits. At some point, the nation as a whole is going to come to the conclusion we have to have competition and choice to help our children succeed.

Q: Are other states following Minnesota's lead?

A: Oh yes, quite a few. California, Ohio, Pennsylvania, New York, Indiana, Illinois. It's growing.

Q: What kind of challenges do you see facing higher education in the future?

A: When you compare Minnesota's higher education institutions to others around the country, we compare very favorably. But the rapid increase in the cost of higher education has made it difficult for the average family to afford to send a child to college. At the same time, the bachelor's degree has become so common, questions have been raised about its value. What we are trying to do in Minnesota is focus on the technical value of any degree. The University of Minnesota, under the leadership of President [Mark] Yudof, has made it clear that it wants to become a premier institution for teaching and research. I have no doubt they will do that, but we still have to come to grips with the issue of rising costs. You can't just look to government and say we have to make more and more money available.

Q: One thing I have thought about a lot as we've researched this book is the interesting political position you have been in during both terms in office. Most of the Republicans in the legislature are more conservative than you are. The Republican party has never supported you. You have always faced a legislature led by Democrats. My question is, in that environment, how were you able to accomplish anything at all?

A: We in Minnesota are a microcosm of what is happening nationally. Moderates in both parties feel increasingly disenfranchised. You have to lean to the far right to appease Republicans or to the far left for Democrats. So, I'm thankful we have primaries.

What we have done in the administration—really from day one—is build coalitions of support for issues and these have been floating coalitions. I really give our staff enormous credit for the painstaking work they have done in building these coalitions. We also decided early on to work with people not just on the basis of their traditional political affiliations, but also on their interests. So we worked right off the bat with people who have interests that involve the great outdoors, those who fish, those who hunt, those who snowmobile. All those interests we brought together and they have become part of a political group. We did the same thing with all the different business interests. And then, we merged those groups. It worked out remarkably well, but I would underscore the tremendous work the staff does in keeping these coalitions intact and building the coalitions necessary to pass legislation.

Q: Several people have said that one key to your legislative success has been Senate Majority Leader Roger Moe. He's been majority leader the entire two terms and, despite significant policy differences, you two have been able to make deals. Would you agree?

A: Yes. I like the old type of politician and that would include the Iron Rangers or people like Roger Moe. You can make deals with them.

Q: Your other legislative tool clearly has been the veto, which you used 179 times. Why?

A: I never understood when I was a legislator and auditor why governors did not use the veto more often. That always perplexed me. In baseball terms, it would be like saying we're not going to use the bunt, or we're not going to try for the home run. You use every single weapon you have. Bear in mind, there are 201 legislators and many of them don't want me to succeed. I use every power I have, whether it is informal power like the bully pulpit or the majesty of the office, or formal power, like the veto.

Q: Do you think future governors will veto more?

A: Yes. Clinton is vetoing left and right, or threatening to. They'll use the veto because it can be used to shape policy in a way that benefits them.

Q: You also have used the veto, especially line-item vetoes of pet projects, to deliver messages to legislators who were particularly uncooperative.

A: Democracy is designed to be controversial. It's designed to get people's juices flowing. If you want a fluid government where everybody thinks alike and looks alike and acts alike, then you have a dictatorship. But if you want people to represent interests that may be different from the majority, then you have a democratic structure. Frankly, I enjoy the fight.

Q: Let's talk a bit about style. One person who has worked with you over many years said that "shrinking violets need not apply," with Governor Carlson. True?

A: Sure, that's part of the fun. By and large, when you hire staff, you're hiring people at far less pay than the private sector. The only reason I can see for anybody to get into that is because they believe very strongly in public policy and they want to see that public policy comes to fruition, to have meaning. And that does involve a contest of wills.

Q: Many people say you have grown a great deal as governor. How do you think you have grown?

A: I think you get more acclimated to the job, and the more acclimated you are, the more comfortable you are in doing it. It's hard psychologically to accept that your name and persona are instantly recognized, whether you're in the hardware store or at a Gopher's game. You get used to it, but it takes time.

Q: What particular strengths do you think you brought to the job initially?

A: I think I was always good at public policy, and I'd like to think I have a fairly good grasp of where public opinion is. It's been hard for me to be as patient as the system requires. There's a lot of interruption and interference. That's the problem with democracy. It's slow going and sometimes awkward.

Q: You mentioned earlier that you try to stay focused on just a few issues and let the rest go. That is, you don't personally concern yourself with things other than your priorities. Why has that been effective?

A: The media would like you to get into every single controversy and your inclination is to do that. "Oh, governor, what do you think of the flag controversy? What do you think of the problems of this group or that group?" You begin to realize you can't manage everything, and you are far better off to just limit yourself to a specific agenda. With me, that agenda has always been finances and the prevention agenda, which includes health care, welfare reform, education, and children's issues.

Q: To limit yourself like that must be difficult sometimes. You have to let go of issues.

A: Let go, and you've got to be disciplined.

Q: It also requires that you have a lot of faith in your agency heads and commissioners who will be addressing the issues that you are not. True?

A: That's right. Not all commissioners are on the frontline. I've been blessed with many wonderful commissioners. Some commissioners you are in contact with daily, like the person in charge of finance. We were really blessed. John Gunyou was superb, and then his assistant Laura King took over. She was great. Then finally, Wayne Simoneau. All of them did an excellent job. Peter Gillette was brilliant at trade and economic development. His advice on a lot of things was very important to me. He really developed the strategy behind our trips abroad. He insisted we go abroad and he was right. Jay Novak has continued his work and has been a marvelous person to work with. Dolores Fridge— the work she did with Tim Sullivan and Todd Johnson and Susan Heegaard on school choice I will never forget. That was an unbeatable team. I remember Dolores in the Governor's Reception Room challenging the legislators on school choice. I'll always love her for that. She ate them alive. We have a wonderful team at [the Department of] Corrections. Janet Entzel is someone I knew from the legislature. I loved her then, I love her now. And, Fred LeFleur, and Janet—they were a wonderful team at corrections. We would not have gotten the boarding school without them. Dave Gruenes at Commerce was very steady, very competent. There's a person who could become governor. We also had a very good staff. The public really should know that we have a lot of very good people in government that have shared their expertise and done extraordinarily well.

Q: What has been your biggest disappointment as governor?

A: I would say the one that hurt the most was the enormous battering we took during the entire year of 1991. It didn't revolve around any one issue, but it was constant. I remember getting up at 2:00 or 3:00 in the morning and wandering around the Governor's Residence and coming to the conclusion that I would be regarded as the worst governor in the history of the state. It was just dreadful.

Q: When I asked people to list disappointments, they often mention the failure to veto the redistricting legislation in 1991. Did that hurt you badly?

A: We sure didn't do it on purpose. Fortunately, we have been able to work with the Democrats in the legislature.

Q: Another failure people list is your inability to move the Republican Party more to the center. What more could you have done?

A: I'm not sure any governor—or any elected official—can control the party. I don't appoint the party chair, like the president appoints the chair of his party. Both political parties have been taken over by outside groups.

Q: Do you advocate getting rid of the caucus system?

A: It's a preposterous system. It's totally outdated. I'd replace it with a primary and do the primary sometime in May or June.

Q: You mentioned the failure to pass a Twins stadium bill as a disappointment. Why did that happen here?

A: There's a growing suspicion and distrust of professional sports. The misbehavior by athletes, the high salaries, and then the taxpayers being asked to fund a sports stadium all are part of it. I think several things need to happen. First, professional sports needs to do something to bring their costs under control. The salaries are excessive. The worst part is, these owners are all supposed to be successful in business. Then why do they keep losing money? Regardless of that, I think it would be a terrible mistake for Minnesota to lose the Twins and I'm hoping we'll come up with a facility plan that deals with the University of Minnesota as well as the Vikings and the Twins.

Q: If the next governor asked for advice about the Twins stadium, what would you say?

A: I don't think I'm the best person to give advice on that. But there's no reason why it can't work out. There really isn't.

Q: Tell me about the role of the first lady. Has she influenced your thinking on public policy?

A: When I was a college student I had a chance to have supper with Eleanor Roosevelt and one of my professors. She was a marvelous, marvelous lady. Part of her greatness was the fact that she understood the power of the first lady in terms of public policy. She didn't see her power as coming from how much she was going to influence her husband as much as that she could influence public opinion directly. That was so important. Susan has had more of a public policy influence than any first lady in state history. But she has done it in a very quiet way. She's very methodical. She's built coalitions and she's very influential on the state's children's agenda. The Action for Children report she and Ron James and Linda Kohl (then state planning director) put together was fabulous. It was the blueprint for state policy on children.

Q: Her work in 1997 and 1998 made Minnesota a leader in working with children and families affected by fetal alcohol syndrome. Will that work continue?

A: I hope so. I would argue that alcohol has a profound effect on our culture and society. Susan saw the effects in the courtroom with children suffering from this disease. Maybe the effect shows up in marital discord, or in the crime rate, or in children's performance in school. We have to deal with it.

Q: If you could sit down with the next governor, what advice would you give him?

A: Orville Freeman once told me that he wished he'd had more fun. And, Wendell Anderson met with me and said, "Be sure to have fun." I don't know if the words "fun" and "governor" go together. We have had fun though, especially some of the events at the Governor's Residence, and we've tried to do fun things. I would tell the next governor though to always keep an eye on the long term. I think that was one of the better things we did do. We recognized in 1991 that we were not going to get a lot of short-term benefit from anything, so we tried to do the long-term planning right. That paid off. There is a tendency with political figures to fall into the short-term trap. They'll have good news for the next couple of months and figure that will buy them time. That's wrong. You're better off seizing the moment, and taking the short-term hits earlier rather than procrastinating.

Q: What do the next 10 years hold for Arne Carlson?

A: Well, I have a 15-year-old daughter, and I'd like to see her be able to go to college and maybe graduate school. She's a good student. I have financial obligations. So, I plan to work in business and volunteer on behalf of school choice. I also want to do some volunteer teaching.

Q: What will you miss about being governor?

A: I think I'll miss being at the center of public policy. And the free parking.

Q: Will you be active in politics at all in the year 2000?

A: If somebody wants me to help out, I'll be tickled pink. I'm going to be advancing the cause of Elizabeth Dole. She'd be terrific.

Q: Any chance of a Dole-Carlson ticket?

A: No. She'd be marvelous though. She'd break the gender barrier and I think she would focus the debate in 2000 on opportunity and equalizing opportunity. I think we have a tendency as a society to want to guarantee outcomes. We can't do that. We can guarantee opportunity. I would like to see that be the political debate of 2000.

Q: Any final thoughts as you leave office?

A: We've had a wonderful life here. We have a wonderful staff at the residence and at the office. It's been a treat for the family. Both [older daughter] Anne [Carlson Davis] and [son] Tucker have lived here [at the residence] for a little while. Both of them celebrated their marriages here. Jessica has been great. She really grew up as part of the first family, and she's never caused us any trouble. Somebody once said that when you die you never regret not spending more time at the office. All of us have to keep that in perspective. You've got to spend quality time with the family. For us, these years have been wonderful and we're very grateful for them.

CARLSON ADMINISTRATION ACCOMPLISHMENTS

Stable Finances, Education Spending, Environmental Protection

- Put Minnesota's financial house in order.

- Turned a $1.8 billion deficit into a $2.3 billion surplus in fiscal year 1997; $1.9 billion in fiscal year 1998.

- Held average growth of state spending (5 percent) below the average rate of growth in personal income (5.4 percent) throughout administration and until 2001.

- Funded nearly $3 billion dollars in tax cuts with the 1998 tax bill.

- Cast 179 vetoes, blocking some $1.5 billion in new taxes, spending, and fees—Governor Carlson has vetoed more bills than all other governors combined since 1939.

- Restored the AAA bond rating from all three rating agencies. Minnesota is now one of only eight states which has earned the top rating by all three of Wall Street's major bond houses and the first such state to receive the upgrade in 25 years. Standard and Poor's credits Minnesota with a level of fiscal management rare among states.

• Replenished and increased state reserves in the amount of more than $2.2 billion. This includes state budget reserves and school-related tax shifts.

• Fostered strong state economic climate.

• Developed a Minnesota economy that is outperforming the nation's.

• Grew personal income in Minnesota by 40 percent since 1991 (15 percent higher than personal income growth nationwide during the same time period).

• Created 394,400 new jobs. Minnesota is growing jobs 50 percent faster than the rest of the nation. The state's unemployment rate is half the national average.

• Increased Minnesota's manufacturing job base 10 percent, compared with the national average that has decreased 4 percent.

• Established an international trade growth rate in Minnesota that is twice as fast as the United States (13 percent versus 6.5 percent).

• Operated 35 Workforce Centers in Minnesota, with plans to open approximately 20 more. Minnesota's Workforce Center system is held up as the national model for one-stop employment centers. The Workforce Centers provide a seamless and comprehensive system for job seekers and employers.

• Reformed the cost drivers: health care, welfare, and workers' compensation. The MinnestotaCare program enrolled 100,000

Minnesotans, including more than 54,000 children who previously had no health insurance. Forty-six hundred fewer families are relying on welfare, saving some $2.2 million each month.

- Moved 52 percent of the Minnesota Family Investment Program's (MFIP) long-term welfare recipients into jobs, an increase of 40 percent compared to the control group of public assistance recipients.

- Decreased Minnesota's welfare caseload by 23 percent since 1994.

- Reduced workers' compensation premiums by 35 percent, saving employers $121 million since 1995, and saving employers $10 million a month.

- Reduced the cost of workers' compensation to approximately $1.19 billion [1996 cost], down from the 1995 estimate of $1.36 billion.

- Returned about $900,000 to approximately 8,000 families who were eligible, but did not apply for, Minnesota's Working Family Tax Credit in December 1997.

- Institutionalized budget reforms.

- Established formal four- and six-year planning horizons. Minnesota's budget is in structural balance until the year 2001.

- Disciplined revenue and expenditure forecasting, indexing state spending to growth in personal income.

- Initiated system of strategic capital budget planning.

- Enacted education reforms, including significant tax cuts.

- Minnesota is the first state to enact statewide education reform involving real school choice, statewide testing, increased funding, and charter and lab schools. Wisconsin has proposed reforms based on the Minnesota model and a number of other states are looking at implementing plans based on what is being called a national educational reform model.

STATEWIDE TESTING

- Enabled all Minnesota parents to determine how their children and their schools are performing.

- Produced results through competition, choice, and accountability. With the 1998 eighth grade basic-skills test results already in, there was an increase from 59 percent passing in 1997 to 68 percent passing in 1998 in reading.

- Produced gains in math that have been slower, but they are being made with an increase from 70 percent passing in 1997 to 71 percent passing in 1998.

PUBLIC SCHOOL FUNDING INCREASE

- Increased spending in the 1997 education reform package by 15 percent to nearly $1 billion over the next biennium. (Total education budget equalled $6 billion.)

- Increased per student spending from $3,505 to $3,660.

- Increased compensatory revenue for low-income students by $100 million.

- Allotted $70 million to implement graduation standards in the 1998 K-12 packages.

- Targeted funds totaling $127 million for important school improvements through the 1998 K-12 bill. The bill provided $54.8 million for graduation standards implementation. An additional $15.9 million went to provide equity for certain districts with low property tax values.

- Dedicated $12 million to establish three residential academies meant to serve children between grades 7 and 12 who have demonstrated a desire to learn but cannot function, for one reason or another, in a traditional classroom setting. The academies are designed to give children one more chance before entering the criminal justice system.

- Designated $14 million in K-12 funding in 1998 for repairs to schools damaged in the 1997 floods, including $7.4 million for East Grand Forks.

EDUCATION TAX DEDUCTIONS

- More than doubled educational tax deduction from $650 to $1,625 for students in grades K-6, and from $1,000 to $2,500 for students in grades 7-12 in 1997.

- Specified deductible items to now include:
  - private school tuition
  - textbooks and instructional materials
  - transportation expenses
  - home computer software and hardware
  - tutoring
  - educational summer school and camps

- Created an educational tax credit for families with incomes below $33,500.

- Created a tax credit of $1,000 per child with a $2,000 limit per family.

- Qualified all items listed above as deductible items except tuition at non-public schools.

SITE-BASED MANAGEMENT

- Delegated funding and decision making to schools rather than districts.

- Empowered schools and parents to decide how resources were to be used at individual schools.

CHARTER SCHOOLS

- Strengthened the opportunities for charter schools to succeed and provide unique learning opportunities for more students. In May 1998, Minnesota had 34 charter schools approved for operation.

LAB SCHOOLS

- Established a lab school grant program linking K-12 and higher education, and enabling new lab schools to test the very best educational practices.

TECHNOLOGY

- Appropriated $90 million to put Minnesota on track to become the lead state in educational technology offering the lowest computer-to-student ratio in the nation.

EXPANSION OF MINNESOTA'S WORKING FAMILY TAX CREDIT

- Expanded the working family tax credit, an existing program designed to allow low- and moderate- income families to keep more of their tax dollars.

- Provided an average increase of $200 to $350 for families making $29,000 or less.

- Allowed for credit to be used for any purpose including non-public school tuition.

- Increased credit from 15 percent to 25 percent of the Federal Earned Income Tax Credit.

- Awarded the Leadership in Educational Choice Award by the Friedman Foundation in 1997 for Governor Carlson's efforts in educational choice.

HIGHER EDUCATION

- Proposed and secured passage of a historic capital improvement package for higher education in 1998. The University of Minnesota received $206 million for projects including a new Molecular and Cellular Biology Building and renovations to Walter Library among other projects.

- Awarded MnSCU a record $155 million from the 1998 bonding bill for systemwide remodeling and facilities enhancement throughout the system.

- Increased funding for the University of Minnesota 18 percent and funding for all institutions 21 percent from fiscal years 1991 to 1999.

- Created U of M "blue chip faculty recruitment pool" to retain and recruit the best and brightest in academia.

- Increased funding for the U of M Academic Health Center, technology transfer, and medical education and research.

ENVIRONMENT

- Signed, in 1998, the largest environmental package in Minnesota history called "Access to the Outdoors." The $140 million package included funds to enhance every park in the state with new and improved trails and expanded wildlife habitat, and nearly $32 million for many other projects, including flood control and mitigation.

- Appropriated more than $2.3 billion for environmental initiatives since 1991.

- Signed into law in 1997 nearly $20 million for contamination cleanup and improvement of industrial polluted lands known as "brownfields."

- Announced a 10-year, multiagency plan to clean up the Minnesota River, and sediment in the river has already been reduced by 25 percent.

- Presented with the Great Blue Heron Award by the North American Waterfowl Management Plan for commitment to wildlife and natural resource preservation.

- Provided more incentive and flexibility in managing wetlands with the landmark Wetlands Act of 1991, giving local governments more authority to develop their plans rather than have the state handle each case individually.

AGRICULTURE
- Developed Minnesota's agricultural economy, which is one quarter of Minnesota's total economy, producing $7 billion worth of products annually.

- Developed Minnesota's agribusiness industry to the seventh largest in the nation with annual international exports of $2.4 billion.

TECHNOLOGY
- Enabled Minnesota to be ranked 14th in the nation in technology-related businesses with more than 2,300 computer-related companies, which employ some 75,000 people and pay $3 billion in wages annually.

- Awarded the Friend to Technology in Public Service Award by the Minnesota High Technology Council in 1997.

MEDICAL TECHNOLOGY

- Developed a $2 billion industry with more than 500 medical product firms employing 17,000 people, ranking Minnesota second in the nation.

- Supported companies such as Medtronic, St. Jude Medical, and 3M, and the University of Minnesota and the Mayo Clinic, sustaining Minnesota's national and international reputation as a leader in medical technology and delivery.

- Awarded Governor of the Year Award by the Biotechnology Industry Organization for efforts in the field of biotechnology.

CRIME

- Signed an unprecedented $976 million crime package that focused efforts on crime prevention, enforcement, corrections, and our judicial system. The goals of the 1997 package were to reverse the disturbing trend of violent juvenile crime, significantly reduce the rate of repeat offenses, target first-time offenders, and enforce all laws, even for the smallest crimes.

Provisions included:

- After-school Enrichment Programs, which provide at-risk youth with more creative and educational activities between the time school lets out and when they go home.

- Weekend Work Camp, located at Camp Ripley, a highly structured work experience for first- and second-time juvenile offenders. This became fully operational in early 1998.

- Wilderness Endeavors, located at the Thistledew Camp. The program uses high adventure to improve the personal growth and development of participants.

- Juvenile Support Network, an after-care service for juveniles that leave residential and correctional facilities.

- Drug and Night Courts, which give the courts further options to deal expeditiously with drug and criminal offenders.

- Gang Strike Task Force, which works with statewide law enforcement and the Bureau of Criminal Apprehension to aggressively target gangs in Minnesota.

- Crime Computer Network, which ensures that law enforcement computers throughout the state are able to interface and share information.

EARLY CHILDHOOD AND FAMILY EDUCATION

- Signed into law the largest appropriation in state history, nearly $400 million for the 1998–99 biennium, in May 1997 for family and early childhood programs. Funding was significantly increased for programs such as:

- Head Start, a family-centered and community-based program that provides developmentally appropriate activities for children and support for parents in their work and child-rearing roles.

- Sliding-Fee Child-Care Program, the funding for which covers an additional 5,500 Minnesota families who are currently on county waiting lists for this program.

- Increased funding for Adult Basic Education, After-school Enrichment, and Learning Readiness.

- Included provision in the bill for at-home infant child care, which allows parents who stay at home with an infant in the first year access to basic sliding-fee child-care funds.

- Appropriated another $163 million for children and family programs in the 1998–99 biennium, including $37.5 million for Head Start, $96 million for the Sliding-Fee Child-Care Program, and nearly $30 million for Early Childhood Family Education.

ACKNOWLEDGMENTS

Every book is a collaborative effort, but few as much as this one. Eight writers contributed to this book. They interviewed about 160 people familiar with the issues and events described here. They also reviewed thousands of pages of documents and newspaper articles to pull together a fair representation of the Carlson years. The writers and their contributions are as follows:

- Mary Lahr Schier (Introduction, Chapters 1, 2, 3, 4, 7, 11, 14, and Epilogue)
- Kate Peterson (Chapters 5 and 6)
- Vicki Stavig (Chapter 8)
- Sara Gilbert (Chapter 9)
- Phil Davies (Chapter 10)
- Marc Hequet (Chapter 12)
- Tracy Baumann (Chapter 13)
- Julie Jensen (Chapter 15)

This could not have been accomplished without the assistance of many people in and outside of the Carlson Administration. Several members of the governor's staff made this book possible by providing information and access. The writers wish to thank especially Bernie Omann, Jackie Renner, Tanja Kozicky, Susan Kalpak, Barbara Hoffmann, Kate Chalmers, Amy Rudolph, and Aimee Kane. Commissioners Jay Novak and Wayne Simoneau provided unique insight and unfailing support for this project. We thank them sincerely.

Many members of the Minnesota Legislature assisted writers as they pieced together events and issues. Special thanks go to Senate Majority Leader Roger Moe, who was accessible to the book's writers during a busy legislative session, and to former Senate Minority Leader Duane Benson, who provided context and details on the early years.

This book would not have been written without the enthusiasm of several of the governor's long-time supporters. The book's writers would like to thank Wheelock Whitney, Kathy Kingman, Rick Nelson, Barry Lazarus, and Lars Carlson, who have led the Minnesota Gubernatorial History Foundation, which funded this project. Lars Carlson also contributed immeasurably to this project by providing insights gained during a lifetime with the governor.

Editors at MSP Communications worked tirelessly to shape the manuscript into a more coherent tale. The writers wish to acknowledge the assistance of Brooke Benson, Doug Benson, Dave Elmstrom, and Tom Mason.

Finally, great thanks go to Governor Arne Carlson, who opened his administration and his mind to the book's writers. We thank him for his cooperation, his honesty, his time, and his willingness to discuss even the most unpleasant aspects of his terms as governor. This is the first history of his administration. We do not think it will be the last.